2025

The Quick

Ninja Foodi

PossibleCooker

COOKBOOK

2000 Days Super Easy, Tasty and Effortless Recipes Book for Families, Featuring Step-by-Step Guides for Flavorful Meals Every Day

Simyukoona Plichtovturt

TABLE OF CONTENTS

Introduction

Chapter 1   Breakfasts   / 5

Chapter 2   Beans and Grains   / 14

Chapter 3   Beef, Pork, and Lamb   / 20

Chapter 4   Fish and Seafood   / 30

Chapter 5   Poultry   / 40

Chapter 6   Stews and Soups   / 51

Chapter 7   Snacks and Appetizers   / 62

Chapter 8   Vegetables and Sides   / 69

Chapter 9   Desserts   / 77

Appendix 1:   Measurement Conversion Chart   / 84

Appendix 2:   Recipes Index   / 85

INTRODUCTION

In the ever-evolving world of cooking appliances, few innovations have sparked as much excitement as the Ninja Foodi PossibleCooker. This remarkable device is not just a pressure cooker or a Ninja Foodi PossibleCooker; it combines multiple cooking methods into one versatile appliance, making it an invaluable addition to any kitchen. With the ability to sauté, steam, air fry, bake, and even slow cook, the PossibleCooker redefines what home cooks can achieve with a single tool.

Unleashing Culinary Creativity

The Ninja Foodi PossibleCooker empowers you to create a wide variety of dishes with ease and efficiency. Imagine transforming ordinary ingredients into extraordinary meals with just the push of a button. Whether you are preparing a hearty stew, perfectly roasted vegetables, or crispy fried chicken, this appliance allows you to do it all in one pot, minimizing cleanup and maximizing flavor. The ability to pressure cook your ingredients locks in moisture and flavor, then finish them off with a crispy air fry, elevates your cooking game like never before. This cookbook is designed to help you harness the full potential of your PossibleCooker, making cooking not only easier but also more enjoyable.

One of the primary goals of this cookbook is to inspire creativity in the kitchen. Many home cooks often find themselves stuck in a rut, preparing the same meals over and over again. With the Ninja Foodi PossibleCooker, you have the opportunity to break free from these patterns and explore new flavors, textures, and cooking techniques. Each recipe has been crafted to highlight the unique capabilities of the PossibleCooker, encouraging you to experiment and discover the joy of cooking again.

Recipes for Every Palate

As you delve into the recipes, you will find that they cater to a variety of tastes and dietary preferences. Whether you are a meat lover, vegetarian, or vegan, this cookbook has something for everyone. The recipes range from comforting classics like beef stew and macaroni and cheese to innovative dishes such as Moroccan-inspired tagines or Asian-style noodle stir-fries. Each recipe includes clear instructions and tips to ensure your cooking experience is seamless and rewarding.

Many of the recipes offer variations and substitutions, allowing you to customize them to suit your preferences and dietary needs. For instance, if you prefer a vegetarian twist on a classic meat dish, you'll find suggestions on how to replace protein sources without sacrificing taste or texture. This flexibility ensures that anyone can enjoy the delicious outcomes from the PossibleCooker, fostering an inclusive cooking experience that encourages everyone to enjoy home-cooked meals together.

A Focus on Convenience and Efficiency

Cooking with the Ninja Foodi PossibleCooker is not just about the end result; it is about the journey. It is an opportunity to gather around the table with family and friends, sharing delicious meals and creating lasting memories. This cookbook encourages you to engage with the cooking process, savoring each step from preparation to plating. Cooking should be a joyous activity, and with the PossibleCooker, it is easier than ever to create dishes that will impress your loved ones.

Moreover, the PossibleCooker's multifunctionality makes it an ideal choice for busy lifestyles. In today's fast-paced world, finding the time to cook can be a challenge. This appliance streamlines the cooking process, allowing you to prepare meals quickly without sacrificing quality or flavor. With features like programmable cooking times and automatic pressure release, the PossibleCooker takes the guesswork out of cooking, enabling you to focus on what truly matters: enjoying your meal.

Mastering the PossibleCooker

In this cookbook, you will also find helpful tips on how to make the most out of your Ninja Foodi PossibleCooker. From understanding the different cooking functions to mastering the art of meal prep, we aim to equip you with the knowledge you need to feel confident in your cooking abilities. Each section includes essential techniques that will elevate your culinary skills and help you make the most of your time in the kitchen.

Understanding the fundamentals of using the PossibleCooker will empower you to take control of your cooking. You will learn how to properly season and prepare ingredients, which will significantly enhance the flavors of your dishes. Each section also includes useful cooking tips, such as how to avoid common mistakes, achieve optimal cooking times, and ensure even cooking throughout your meal. We also provide insights into ingredient substitutions, so you can create meals tailored to your personal taste or dietary restrictions.

Embracing the Joy of Cooking

As you explore the pages of this cookbook, we encourage you to embrace the spirit of experimentation. Feel free to mix and match ingredients, try new flavor combinations, and make the recipes your own. Cooking is a personal expression of creativity, and we hope that the recipes within these pages inspire you to discover your unique culinary voice.

The Ninja Foodi PossibleCooker is not just an appliance; it is a gateway to endless culinary possibilities. Its unique combination of functions allows you to tackle everything from weeknight dinners to festive feasts with ease. Picture yourself hosting a gathering with family and friends, confidently serving a delicious meal that you prepared with little effort thanks to your PossibleCooker.

Conclusion: Let's Get Cooking!

As you embark on this journey through the pages of this cookbook, we hope you find joy in every meal you create. With the help of the PossibleCooker, the kitchen will become a space of innovation, exploration, and fun. You will find that cooking is not just about the food; it is about the love, creativity, and connection that each meal brings to the table.

So, roll up your sleeves, gather your ingredients, and get ready to embark on a delicious adventure with your Ninja Foodi PossibleCooker. Whether you are a seasoned chef or a novice cook, this cookbook is designed to help you unlock the full potential of this incredible appliance. Let's get cooking, and may every dish be a reflection of your culinary journey and a celebration of the flavors that bring us all together!

Chapter

1

Breakfasts

Chapter 1 Breakfasts

Crunchy Keto Nut Granola

Prep time: 10 minutes | Cook time: 3 to 4 hours | Serves 16

- ½ cup coconut oil, melted
- 2 teaspoons pure vanilla extract
- 1 teaspoon maple extract
- 1 cup chopped pecans
- 1 cup sunflower seeds
- 1 cup unsweetened shredded
- coconut
- ½ cup hazelnuts
- ½ cup slivered almonds
- ¼ cup granulated erythritol
- ½ teaspoon cinnamon
- ¼ teaspoon ground nutmeg
- ¼ teaspoon salt

1. Lightly grease the insert of the Ninja Foodi PossibleCooker with 1 tablespoon of the coconut oil. 2. In a large bowl, whisk together the remaining coconut oil, vanilla, and maple extract. Add the pecans, sunflower seeds, coconut, hazelnuts, almonds, erythritol, cinnamon, nutmeg, and salt. Toss to coat the nuts and seeds. 3. Transfer the mixture to the insert. 4. Cover and cook on low for 3 to 4 hours, until the granola is crispy. 5. Transfer the granola to a baking sheet covered in parchment or foil to cool. 6. Store in a sealed container in the refrigerator for up to 2 weeks.

Basic Strata

Prep time: 10 minutes | Cook time: 4½ hours | Serves 8 to 10

- 8 cups torn or cubed (1-inch) stale bread, tough crusts removed
- 3½ to 4 cups shredded cheese
- 10 large eggs
- 3 cups milk
- 1½ teaspoons salt
- ½ teaspoon hot sauce
-

1. Lightly grease the interior of a 5- to 7-quart Ninja Foodi PossibleCooker with nonstick cooking spray or use a slow-cooker liner, following the instructions provided by the manufacturer.2. Arrange a portion of the bread pieces in an even layer inside the Ninja Foodi PossibleCooker, then scatter a generous amount of cheese over the top. Keep layering the bread and cheese alternately until all ingredients are used, reserving a small amount of cheese for the final topping.3. In a large mixing bowl, combine the eggs, milk, salt, and hot sauce, and whisk thoroughly until smooth. Pour this egg mixture evenly over the layered bread and cheese, pressing down gently to ensure the bread is fully soaked. Finish by sprinkling the remaining cheese on top.4. Cover the Ninja Foodi PossibleCooker and set it to low heat, cooking for 4 hours or until the strata reaches 170°F (77°C) when tested with an instant-read thermometer. Uncover and continue cooking for an extra 30 minutes to firm up.5. Keep the strata warm in the Ninja Foodi PossibleCooker until ready to serve, and dish out portions directly from the cooker.

Croque Monsieur Strata

Prep time: 10 minutes | Cook time: 4½ hours | Serves 8

- 8 large eggs
- 2 cups whole or low-fat milk
- 6 shakes Tabasco sauce
- 1 tablespoon Dijon mustard
- 8 cups torn soft-crusted French bread (if the crust is crispy, remove it and use the
- center of the bread)
- 8 ounces (227 g) sliced Black Forest ham, cut into matchsticks
- 3 cups shredded Gruyère cheese
- 4 tablespoons (½ stick) unsalted butter, melted

1. Lightly grease the inside of a 5- to 7-quart Ninja Foodi PossibleCooker with nonstick cooking spray or line it with a slow-cooker liner, following the manufacturer's instructions.2. In a large bowl, whisk together the eggs, milk, Tabasco, and mustard until well combined. Add the bread cubes and diced ham, stirring to make sure the bread is fully soaked and the ham is evenly distributed.3. Spoon half of the soaked bread mixture into the prepared Ninja Foodi PossibleCooker, spreading it out evenly. Sprinkle half of the shredded cheese over the top. Repeat the layering with the remaining bread mixture and cheese, then drizzle the melted butter over everything.4. Cover and set the Ninja Foodi PossibleCooker to low, cooking for about 4 hours, or until the strata reaches an internal temperature of 170°F (77°C) and is firm. Remove the lid and cook for an additional 30 minutes to finish setting.5. Keep the strata warm in the Ninja Foodi PossibleCooker until ready to serve, and dish out portions directly from the cooker.

Golden Granola

Prep time: 15 minutes | Cook time: 4 hours | Makes 8 cups

- Nonstick cooking spray
- 4 cups old-fashioned rolled oats
- 1 cup slivered almonds
- 1 cup coarsely chopped pecans
- 1 cup sunflower seeds
- 1 cup shredded coconut
- ⅓ cup butter or coconut oil
- 2 tablespoons safflower oil
- ½ cup honey
- ⅓ cup brown sugar
- 2 teaspoons vanilla
- 1 teaspoon ground cinnamon
- ½ teaspoon salt

1. Spray the Ninja Foodi PossibleCooker with the nonstick cooking spray. 2. In the Ninja Foodi PossibleCooker, combine the oats, almonds, pecans, sunflower seeds, and coconut. 3. In a medium saucepan over low heat, heat the butter, safflower oil, honey, brown sugar, vanilla, cinnamon, and salt until the butter melts, about 5 minutes. 4. Drizzle the butter mixture over the ingredients in the Ninja Foodi PossibleCooker and stir to coat. 5. Cover, but leave the lid slightly ajar, and cook on low for 3 to 4 hours, stirring every hour if possible, until the mixture is golden brown. 6. Remove the granola to greased baking sheets and spread into an even layer. Let cool, and then break into pieces. Serve or store in an airtight container at room temperature.

Fruity Steel-Cut Oatmeal

Prep time: 10 minutes | Cook time: 7½ hours | Serves 2

- Nonstick cooking spray
- 1½ cups steel-cut oats
- ½ cup dried cranberries
- ½ cup golden raisins
- ½ cup chopped dried apricots
- 5 cups water
- 1 cup almond milk
- 3 tablespoons brown sugar
- 2 tablespoons honey
- ½ teaspoon salt
- 2 teaspoons vanilla

1. Coat the Ninja Foodi PossibleCooker generously with nonstick cooking spray.2. Mix together the oats, dried cranberries, raisins, and chopped apricots directly in the Ninja Foodi PossibleCooker, ensuring they are well combined.3. Pour in the water and almond milk, followed by the brown sugar, honey, salt, and vanilla extract, stirring everything until the ingredients are evenly distributed.4. Secure the lid and set the Ninja Foodi PossibleCooker to low heat, letting it cook for 7½ hours, or until the oatmeal reaches a creamy consistency. Serve immediately while warm.

Veggie Omelet

Prep time: 15 minutes | Cook time: 4 to 5 hours | Serves 8

- 1 tablespoon extra-virgin olive oil
- 10 eggs
- ½ cup heavy (whipping) cream
- 1 teaspoon minced garlic
- ¼ teaspoon salt
- ⅛ teaspoon freshly ground black pepper
- ½ cup chopped cauliflower
- ½ cup chopped broccoli
- 1 red bell pepper, chopped
- 1 scallion, white and green parts, chopped
- 4 ounces (113 g) goat cheese, crumbled
- 2 tablespoons chopped parsley, for garnish

1. Lightly grease the insert of the Ninja Foodi PossibleCooker with the olive oil. 2. In a medium bowl, whisk together the eggs, heavy cream, garlic, salt, and pepper. Stir in the cauliflower, broccoli, red bell pepper, and scallion. Pour the mixture into the Ninja Foodi PossibleCooker. Sprinkle the top with goat cheese. 3. Cover and cook on low for 4 to 5 hours. 4. Serve topped with the parsley.

Polenta

Prep time: 10 minutes | Cook time:2 to 9 hours | Serves 8 to 10

- 4 tablespoons melted butter, divided
- ¼ teaspoon paprika
- 6 cups boiling water
- 2 cups dry cornmeal
- 2 teaspoons salt

1. Use 1 tablespoon of butter to thoroughly grease the inside of the Ninja Foodi PossibleCooker, then sprinkle a light dusting of paprika over the bottom. Set the Ninja Foodi PossibleCooker to high heat.2. Add all the remaining ingredients to the Ninja Foodi PossibleCooker, including the extra tablespoon of butter, following the order listed. Stir everything thoroughly to combine.3. Cover and cook on high for 2 to 3 hours, or on low for 6 to 9 hours, making sure to stir occasionally to prevent sticking.4. When the polenta is fully cooked and smooth, transfer it into two loaf pans that have been lightly greased. Refrigerate for at least 8 hours or leave overnight to set.5. To serve, slice the chilled polenta into ¼-inch-thick pieces. Heat 2 tablespoons of butter in a large nonstick skillet, place the slices in, and cook until they are golden brown on one side. Flip and brown the other side.6. For a breakfast option, enjoy with your preferred sweetener or topping.

Garden Veggie Egg Hash

Prep time: 20 minutes | Cook time: 6¼ hours | Serves 2

- Nonstick cooking spray
- 1 onion, chopped
- 2 garlic cloves, minced
- 1 red bell pepper, chopped
- 1 yellow summer squash, chopped
- 2 carrots, chopped
- 2 Yukon Gold potatoes, peeled and chopped
- 2 large tomatoes, seeded and chopped
- ¼ cup vegetable broth
- ½ teaspoon salt
- ⅛ teaspoon freshly ground black pepper
- ½ teaspoon dried thyme leaves
- 3 or 4 eggs
- ½ teaspoon ground sweet paprika

1. Spray the Ninja Foodi PossibleCooker with the nonstick cooking spray. 2. In the Ninja Foodi PossibleCooker, combine all the ingredients except the eggs and paprika, and stir. 3. Cover and cook on low for 6 hours. 4. Uncover and make 1 indentation in the vegetable mixture for each egg. Break 1 egg into a small cup and slip the egg into an indentation. Repeat with the remaining eggs. Sprinkle with the paprika. 5. Cover and cook on low for 10 to 15 minutes, or until the eggs are just set, and serve.

Sausage Quiche

Prep time: 20 minutes | Cook time: 6 hours | Serves 2

- 8 ounces (227 g) pork sausage
- 1 onion, chopped
- 1 cup sliced mushrooms
- Nonstick baking spray containing flour
- 2 garlic cloves, minced
- 1 red bell pepper, chopped
- 1 cup shredded Cheddar cheese, divided
- 4 eggs, beaten
- 1 cup whole milk
- ½ cup all-purpose flour
- ½ teaspoon baking powder
- ½ teaspoon salt
- ½ teaspoon dried basil leaves
- ⅛ teaspoon freshly ground black pepper
- ⅓ cup grated Parmesan cheese

1. In a medium saucepan over medium heat, cook the sausage and chopped onions, stirring frequently to break up the sausage, until it is browned and cooked through, about 10 minutes. Drain off any excess fat and add the sliced mushrooms. Continue cooking and stirring until the mushrooms release their liquid and it evaporates, about 5 minutes.2. Line the inside of the Ninja Foodi PossibleCooker with heavy-duty foil, making sure it covers the sides well. Spray the foil with nonstick baking spray that contains flour to prevent sticking.3. Spread the sausage and mushroom mixture evenly into the bottom of the Ninja Foodi PossibleCooker. Add the minced garlic and chopped bell pepper on top, then sprinkle with ½ cup of shredded Cheddar cheese.4. In a medium bowl, whisk together the eggs, milk, flour, baking powder, salt, dried basil, and black pepper until smooth. Pour this egg mixture over the ingredients in the Ninja Foodi PossibleCooker, making sure it spreads evenly. Top with the remaining ½ cup of Cheddar cheese and sprinkle with grated Parmesan.5. Cover and cook on low for about 6 hours, or until the quiche reaches an internal temperature of 160°F (71°C) and the edges are browned while the center is firm and set.6. Carefully lift the quiche from the Ninja Foodi PossibleCooker using the foil, let it rest for 5 minutes, slice into wedges, and serve warm.

Blueberry Apple Waffle Topping

Prep time: 10 minutes | Cook time: 3 hours | Serves 10 to 12

- 1 quart natural applesauce, unsweetened
- 2 Granny Smith apples, unpeeled, cored, and sliced
- 1 pint fresh or frozen blueberries
- ½ tablespoon ground cinnamon
- ½ cup pure maple syrup
- 1 teaspoon almond flavoring
- ½ cup walnuts, chopped
- Nonfat cooking spray

1. In a Ninja Foodi PossibleCooker coated with nonfat cooking spray, mix together the applesauce, diced apples, and blueberries until well combined.2. Sprinkle in the cinnamon and drizzle the maple syrup over the fruit mixture, stirring to evenly distribute the flavors.3. Cover the Ninja Foodi PossibleCooker with the lid and cook on low for 3 hours, allowing the fruit to soften and the flavors to meld.4. Stir in the almond flavoring and chopped walnuts right before serving for added aroma and crunch.

Overnight Comfort Oats

Prep time: 5 minutes | Cook time: 8 hours | Serves 4 to 5

- 1 cup dry steel-cut oats
- 4 cups water

1. Combine ingredients in Ninja Foodi PossibleCooker. 2. Cover and cook on low overnight, or for 8 hours. 3. Stir before serving. Serve with your other favorite toppings.

Savory Sausage Egg Bake

Prep time: 15 minutes | Cook time: 2 to 2½ hours | Serves 6

- 1 pound (454 g) loose sausage
- 6 eggs
- 1 cup all-purpose baking mix
- 1 cup shredded Cheddar
- cheese
- 2 cups milk
- ¼ teaspoon dry mustard (optional)
- Nonstick cooking spray

1. Brown sausage in nonstick skillet. Break up chunks of meat as it cooks. Drain. 2. Meanwhile, spray interior of Ninja Foodi PossibleCooker with nonstick cooking spray. 3. Mix all ingredients in Ninja Foodi PossibleCooker. 4. Cover and cook on high 1 hour. Turn to low and cook 1 to 1½ hours, or until the dish is fully cooked in the center.

Oatmeal

Prep time: 15 minutes | Cook time: 8 to 9 hours | Serves 7 to 8

- 2 cups dry rolled oats
- 4 cups water
- 1 large apple, peeled and chopped
- 1 cup raisins
- 1 teaspoon cinnamon
- 1 to 2 tablespoons orange zest

1. Add all the ingredients into your Ninja Foodi PossibleCooker, ensuring everything is well mixed.2. Cover with the lid and cook on low for 8 to 9 hours, allowing the flavors to meld and the dish to reach the desired consistency.3. When ready to serve, top with brown sugar if desired and a splash of milk for added richness.

Breakfast Prunes

Prep time: 10 minutes | Cook time: 8 to 10 hours | Serves 6

- 2 cups orange juice
- ¼ cup orange marmalade
- 1 teaspoon ground cinnamon
- ¼ teaspoon ground cloves
- ¼ teaspoon ground nutmeg
- 1 cup water
- 1 (12-ounce / 340-g) package pitted dried prunes
- 2 thin lemon slices

1. Mix the orange juice, marmalade, cinnamon, cloves, nutmeg, and water together in the Ninja Foodi PossibleCooker until well combined.2. Add the prunes and lemon slices, stirring gently to distribute them evenly.3. Cover the Ninja Foodi PossibleCooker and set it to low heat, cooking for 8 to 10 hours, or overnight, until the flavors are fully blended.4. Serve warm as a comforting breakfast, or enjoy it warm or chilled as a flavorful side dish with a meal later in the day.

Huevos Rancheros

Prep time: 10 minutes | Cook time: 3 hours | Serves 8

- 1 tablespoon extra-virgin olive oil
- 10 eggs
- 1 cup heavy (whipping) cream
- 1 cup shredded Monterey Jack cheese, divided
- 1 cup prepared or homemade
- salsa
- 1 scallion, green and white parts, chopped
- 1 jalapeño pepper, chopped
- ½ teaspoon chili powder
- ½ teaspoon salt
- 1 avocado, chopped, for garnish

1 tablespoon chopped cilantro, for garnish

1. Lightly grease the insert of the Ninja Foodi PossibleCooker with the olive oil. 2. In a large bowl, whisk together the eggs, heavy cream, ½ cup of the cheese, salsa, scallion, jalapeño, chili powder, and salt. Pour the mixture into the insert and sprinkle the top with the remaining ½ cup of cheese. 3. Cover and cook until the eggs are firm, about 3 hours on low. 4. Let the eggs cool slightly, then cut into wedges and serve garnished with avocado and cilantro.

Overnight Oatmeal

Prep time: 5 minutes | Cook time: 3 to 10 hours | Serves 8

- 3¾ cups old-fashioned rolled oats
- 8 cups water
- ½ teaspoon salt
- 4 tablespoons (½ stick)
- unsalted butter, cut into small pieces
- 2 cups milk or cream, warmed, for serving
- ¼ cup cinnamon sugar for serving

1. Grease the insert of a 5- to 7-quart Ninja Foodi PossibleCooker with nonstick cooking spray or line it with a slow-cooker liner as directed by the manufacturer.2. Add the oatmeal, water, and salt to the Ninja Foodi PossibleCooker, stirring to combine. Cover and set to cook on low for 8 to 10 hours or on high for 3 to 4 hours, until the oatmeal becomes creamy.3. Once cooked, stir in the butter until melted and well incorporated. Serve hot with warmed milk and a sprinkle of cinnamon sugar for added flavor.

Spiced Pumpkin Pudding

Prep time: 15 minutes | Cook time: 6 to 7 hours | Serves 8

- ¼ cup melted butter, divided
- 2½ cups canned pumpkin purée
- 2 cups coconut milk
- 4 eggs
- 1 tablespoon pure vanilla extract
- 1 cup almond flour
- ½ cup granulated erythritol
- 2 ounces (57 g) protein powder
- 1 teaspoon baking powder
- 1 teaspoon ground cinnamon
- ¼ teaspoon ground nutmeg
- Pinch ground cloves

1. Lightly grease the insert of the Ninja Foodi PossibleCooker with 1 tablespoon of the butter. 2. In a large bowl, whisk together the remaining butter, pumpkin, coconut milk, eggs, and vanilla until well blended. 3. In a small bowl, stir together the almond flour, erythritol, protein powder, baking powder, cinnamon, nutmeg, and cloves. 4. Add the dry ingredients to the wet ingredients and stir to combine. 5. Pour the mixture into the insert. 6. Cover and cook on low for 6 to 7 hours. 7. Serve warm.

Hearty Breakfast Risotto

Prep time: 20 minutes | Cook time: 7 hours | Serves 2

- 8 ounces (227 g) pork sausage
- 1 onion, chopped
- 2 garlic cloves, minced
- Nonstick cooking spray
- 1 cup sliced cremini mushrooms
- 1 cup Arborio rice
- 3 cups chicken stock
- ½ cup milk
- ½ teaspoon salt
- ½ teaspoon dried marjoram leaves
- ⅛ teaspoon freshly ground black pepper
- ⅓ cup grated Parmesan cheese
- 1 tablespoon butter

1. In a medium saucepan over medium heat, cook the sausage, onion, and garlic until the sausage is browned, about 10 minutes, stirring to break up the meat. Drain well. 2. Spray the Ninja Foodi PossibleCooker with the nonstick cooking spray. 3. In the Ninja Foodi PossibleCooker, combine the sausage mixture, mushrooms, and rice. Add the stock, milk, salt, marjoram, and pepper, and stir. 4. Cover and cook on low for 7 hours. 5. Stir in the cheese and butter. Let stand for 5 minutes, and then serve.

Classic Welsh Rarebit Dip

Prep time: 10 minutes | Cook time: 1½ to 2½ hours | Serves 6 to 8

- 1 (12-ounce / 340-g) can beer
- 1 tablespoon dry mustard
- 1 teaspoon Worcestershire sauce
- ½ teaspoon salt
- ⅛ teaspoon black or white pepper
- 1 pound (454 g) American
- cheese, cubed
- 1 pound (454 g) sharp Cheddar cheese, cubed
- English muffins or toast
- Tomato slices
- Bacon, cooked until crisp
- Fresh steamed asparagus spears

1. In Ninja Foodi PossibleCooker, combine beer, mustard, 2. Worcestershire sauce, salt, and pepper. Cover and cook on high 1 to 2 hours, until mixture boils. 3. Add cheese, a little at a time, stirring constantly until all the cheese melts. 4. Heat on high 20 to 30 minutes with cover off, stirring frequently. 5. Serve hot over toasted English muffins or over toasted bread cut into triangles. Garnish with tomato slices, strips of crisp bacon and steamed asparagus spears.

Cinnamon Streusel Slow-Cooker Cake

Prep time: 10 minutes | Cook time: 3 to 4 hours | Serves 8 to 10

- 1 (16-ounce / 454-g) package pound cake mix, prepared according to package directions
- ¼ cup packed brown sugar
- 1 tablespoon flour
- ¼ cup chopped nuts
- 1 teaspoon cinnamon

1. Liberally grease and flour a 2-pound (907-g) coffee can, or Ninja Foodi PossibleCooker baking insert, that fits into your Ninja Foodi PossibleCooker. Pour prepared cake mix into coffee can or baking insert. 2. In a small bowl, mix brown sugar, flour, nuts, and cinnamon together. Sprinkle over top of cake mix. 3. Place coffee tin or baking insert in Ninja Foodi PossibleCooker. Cover top of tin or insert with several layers of paper towels. 4. Cover cooker itself and cook on high 3 to 4 hours, or until toothpick inserted in center of cake comes out clean. 5. Remove baking tin from Ninja Foodi PossibleCooker and allow to cool for 30 minutes before cutting into wedges to serve.

Breakfast Oatmeal

Prep time: 5 minutes | Cook time: 8 hours | Serves 6

- 2 cups dry rolled oats
- 4 cups water
- 1 teaspoon salt
- ½ to 1 cup chopped dates, or raisins, or cranberries, or a mixture of any of these fruits

1. Place all the ingredients into the Ninja Foodi PossibleCooker, making sure they are well combined.2. Cover with the lid and set to cook on low heat overnight, or for approximately 8 hours, until everything is tender and flavors are melded.

Three-Cheese Vegetable Strata

Prep time: 20 minutes | Cook time: 6 hours | Serves 2

- 1 tablespoon extra-virgin olive oil
- 1 tablespoon butter
- 1 onion, chopped
- 2 garlic cloves, minced
- 1½ cups baby spinach leaves
- 1 red bell pepper, chopped
- 1 large tomato, seeded and chopped
- 1 cup cubed ham
- Nonstick cooking spray
- 5 eggs, beaten
- 1 cup milk
- ½ teaspoon salt
- ½ teaspoon dried thyme leaves
- ⅛ teaspoon freshly ground black pepper
- 6 slices French bread, cubed
- 1 cup shredded Cheddar cheese
- ½ cup shredded Swiss cheese
- ¼ cup grated Parmesan cheese

1. In a medium saucepan over medium heat, warm the olive oil and butter. Add the chopped onion and minced garlic, sautéing and stirring frequently until the vegetables become tender, about 6 minutes.2. Stir in the spinach and cook until it wilts, approximately 5 minutes. Take the pan off the heat and mix in the diced bell pepper, chopped tomato, and diced ham.3. Line the Ninja Foodi PossibleCooker with heavy-duty foil, making sure it covers the sides well, and spray generously with nonstick cooking spray.4. In a medium bowl, beat the eggs thoroughly with the milk, salt, thyme, and black pepper until fully combined.5. Begin layering in the Ninja Foodi PossibleCooker: place half of the French bread cubes on the bottom, then add half of the vegetable and ham mixture, followed by half of the shredded Cheddar and Swiss cheeses. Repeat the layering process with the remaining bread, vegetable mixture, and cheeses.6. Evenly pour the egg mixture over the layers, making sure everything is well covered, and then sprinkle with the grated Parmesan cheese.7. Cover and cook on low heat for about 6 hours, or until a food thermometer reads 160°F (71°C) and the egg mixture is set.8. Carefully lift the strata from the Ninja Foodi PossibleCooker using the foil sling, cut into portions, and serve warm.

Sunrise Fruit Compote

Prep time: 5 minutes | Cook time: 2 to 7 hours | Serves 8 to 9

- 1 (12-ounce / 340-g) package dried apricots
- 1 (12-ounce / 340-g) package pitted dried plums
- 1 (11-ounce / 312-g) can mandarin oranges in light
- syrup, undrained
- 1 (29-ounce / 822-g) can sliced peaches in light syrup, undrained
- ¼ cup white raisins
- 10 maraschino cherries

1. Combine all ingredients in Ninja Foodi PossibleCooker. Mix well. 2. Cover. Cook on low 6 to 7 hours, or on high 2 to 3 hours.

Dulce Leche

Prep time: 5 minutes | Cook time: 2 hours | Makes 2½ cups

- 2 (14-ounce / 397-g) cans sweetened condensed milk
- Cookies, for serving

1. Position the unopened cans of milk inside the Ninja Foodi PossibleCooker. Fill the Ninja Foodi PossibleCooker with warm water until it rises 1½ to 2 inches above the tops of the cans.2. Secure the lid on the Ninja Foodi PossibleCooker and set it to high heat. Cook for 2 hours.3. Carefully allow the unopened cans to cool completely.4. Once cooled, open the cans to reveal a thick, spreadable filling perfect for layering between two cookies.

Baked Oatmeal

Prep time: 10 minutes | Cook time: 2½ to 3 hours | Serves 4 to 6

- ⅓ cup oil
- ½ cup sugar
- 1 large egg, beaten
- 2 cups dry quick oats
- 1½ teaspoons baking powder
- ½ teaspoon salt
- ¾ cup milk

1. Pour the oil into the Ninja Foodi PossibleCooker to grease bottom and sides. 2. Add remaining ingredients. Mix well. 3. Cook on low 2½ to 3 hours.

Banana Bread Breakfast Bake

Prep time: 15 minutes | Cook time: 6 hours | Serves 2

- Nonstick cooking spray
- 6 slices banana bread, cubed
- 6 slices French bread, cubed
- 1 banana, sliced
- 4 slices bacon, cooked and crumbled
- ½ cup chopped pecans
- 4 eggs, beaten
- 1½ cups milk
- ⅓ cup sugar
- 2 tablespoons honey
- 1 teaspoon ground cinnamon
- 1 teaspoon vanilla
- ¼ teaspoon salt

1. Spray the Ninja Foodi PossibleCooker with the nonstick cooking spray. 2. In the Ninja Foodi PossibleCooker, layer the banana bread, French bread, banana, bacon, and pecans. 3. In a medium bowl, beat the eggs, milk, sugar, honey, cinnamon, vanilla, and salt. Pour the egg mixture into the Ninja Foodi PossibleCooker. 4. Cover and cook on low for 6 hours, or until the temperature registers 160°F (71°C) on a food thermometer, and serve.

Frittata Provencal

Prep time: 30 minutes | Cook time: 3 hours | Serves 6

- ½ cup water
- 1 tablespoon olive oil
- 1 medium Yukon Gold potato, peeled and sliced
- 1 small onion, thinly sliced
- ½ teaspoon smoked paprika
- 12 eggs
- 1 teaspoon minced fresh thyme or ¼ teaspoon dried
- thyme
- 1 teaspoon hot pepper sauce
- ½ teaspoon salt
- ¼ teaspoon pepper
- 1 (4-ounce / 113-g) log fresh goat cheese, coarsely crumbled, divided
- ½ cup chopped soft sundried tomatoes (not packed in oil)

1. Layer two 24-inch pieces of aluminum foil and fold up one long side to form a 1-inch wide strip. Shape the foil into a coil to create a makeshift rack, and place it at the bottom of a 6-quart oval Ninja Foodi PossibleCooker. Pour in enough water to surround the rack, ensuring it's stable.2. Heat oil in a large skillet over medium-high heat. Add the diced potato and chopped onion, cooking and stirring for 5 to 7 minutes until the potatoes are lightly browned. Sprinkle in the paprika and mix well. Transfer the mixture into a greased 1½-quart baking dish that fits inside the Ninja Foodi PossibleCooker.3. In a large bowl, whisk together the eggs, thyme, hot pepper sauce, salt, and black pepper. Stir in 2 ounces (57 g) of goat cheese. Pour this egg mixture over the potatoes in the baking dish, then top with sliced tomatoes and the remaining goat cheese. Carefully place the dish on top of the foil rack inside the Ninja Foodi PossibleCooker.4. Cover and cook on low heat for 3 hours, or until the eggs are set and a knife inserted near the center comes out clean. Serve warm.

Pumpkin Spice Breakfast Bars

Prep time: 15 minutes | Cook time: 3 hours | Makes 8 bars

Crust:
- 5 tablespoons butter, softened, divided
- ¾ cup unsweetened shredded

Filling:
- 1 (28-ounce / 794-g) can pumpkin purée
- 1 cup heavy (whipping) cream
- 4 eggs
- 1 ounce (28 g) protein powder
- 1 teaspoon pure vanilla

- coconut
- ½ cup almond flour
- ¼ cup granulated erythritol

- extract
- 4 drops liquid stevia
- 1 teaspoon ground cinnamon
- ½ teaspoon ground ginger
- ¼ teaspoon ground nutmeg
- Pinch ground cloves
- Pinch salt

Make the Crust: 1. Lightly grease the bottom of the insert of the Ninja Foodi PossibleCooker with 1 tablespoon of the butter. 2. In a small bowl, stir together the coconut, almond flour, erythritol, and remaining butter until the mixture forms into coarse crumbs. 3. Press the crumbs into the bottom of the insert evenly to form a crust. Make the Filling: 4. In a medium bowl, stir together the pumpkin, heavy cream, eggs, protein powder, vanilla, stevia, cinnamon, ginger, nutmeg, cloves, and salt until well blended. 5. Spread the filling evenly over the crust. 6. Cover and cook on low for 3 hours. 7. Uncover and let cool for 30 minutes. Then place the insert in the refrigerator until completely chilled, about 2 hours. 8. Cut into squares and store them in the refrigerator in a sealed container for up to 5 days.

Chocolate-Cherry–Stuffed French Toast

Prep time: 15 minutes | Cook time: 6 hours | Serves 2

- Nonstick cooking spray
- 8 slices French bread
- ¾ cup mascarpone cheese
- ½ cup cherry preserves
- ¾ cup semisweet chocolate chips, melted
- 1 cup sliced pitted fresh cherries
- 5 eggs, beaten
- 1 cup milk
- 1 teaspoon vanilla
- ½ teaspoon ground cinnamon
- ¼ teaspoon salt

1. Line the inside of the Ninja Foodi PossibleCooker with heavy-duty foil and generously coat it with nonstick cooking spray.2. Spread mascarpone cheese on one side of each slice of bread, followed by a layer of cherry preserves. Drizzle melted chocolate over the preserves.3. Cut each slice of bread in half and arrange the pieces in layers inside the Ninja Foodi PossibleCooker, adding fresh cherries between the bread slices.4. In a medium bowl, whisk together the eggs, milk, vanilla extract, cinnamon, and salt until smooth. Pour the egg mixture evenly over the layered bread and cherries in the Ninja Foodi PossibleCooker.5. Cover and cook on low heat for 6 hours, or until the dish is set and reaches an internal temperature of 160°F (71°C). Use the foil to lift the dessert out of the Ninja Foodi PossibleCooker, slice, and serve warm.

Peach French Toast Bake

Prep time: 15 minutes | Cook time: 6 hours | Serves 2

- Nonstick cooking spray
- ½ cup brown sugar
- 3 tablespoons butter
- 1 tablespoon water
- 1 teaspoon vanilla
- 8 slices French bread
- 1½ cups peeled sliced peaches
- 4 eggs
- 1 cup milk
- ¼ cup granulated sugar
- ½ teaspoon ground cinnamon
- ¼ teaspoon salt
- ⅔ cup chopped pecans

1. Line the inside of the Ninja Foodi PossibleCooker with heavy-duty foil and coat it with nonstick cooking spray to prevent sticking.2. In a small saucepan over low heat, combine the brown sugar, butter, and water. Bring to a simmer, stirring frequently, and let it simmer for about 5 minutes until a thick syrup forms. Remove from heat and stir in the vanilla extract.3. Arrange layers of bread and sliced peaches in the Ninja Foodi PossibleCooker, drizzling each layer with some of the prepared brown sugar syrup to evenly distribute the sweetness.4. In a medium bowl, whisk together the eggs, milk, granulated sugar, cinnamon, and salt until well blended. Pour this egg mixture over the layered bread and peaches, and sprinkle the top with chopped pecans.5. Cover the Ninja Foodi PossibleCooker and set to cook on low for 6 hours, or until the mixture is set and reaches 160°F (71°C) when tested with a food thermometer.6. Carefully remove the dessert from the Ninja Foodi PossibleCooker using the foil, slice into portions, and serve warm.

Chapter

2

Beans and Grains

Chapter 2 Beans and Grains

Cheesy Grits Bake

Prep time: 10 minutes | Cook time: 8 hours | Serves 8

- 1 cup stone-ground grits
- 4½ cups chicken broth
- 4 tablespoons (½ stick) unsalted butter, melted and slightly cooled
- 2 large eggs, beaten
- ½ cup heavy cream
- 2 cup finely shredded mild Cheddar cheese

1. Coat the insert of a Ninja Foodi PossibleCooker with nonstick cooking spray or line it with a slow-cooker liner according to the manufacturer's directions. 2. Stir the grits, broth, and butter together in the slow-cooker insert. Cover and cook on low for 4 hours. Stir in the eggs, cream, and cheese. Cover and cook for an additional 4 hours, until the grits are creamy and the cheese has melted. 3. Serve from the cooker set on warm.

Bulgur and Shiitake Mushroom Pilaf

Prep time: 15 minutes | Cook time: 5 to 6 hours | Serves 8

- 2 cups medium bulgur
- 2 tablespoons extra-virgin olive oil
- 1 medium onion, finely chopped
- 2 cloves garlic, minced
- 8 ounces (227 g) fresh
- shiitake mushrooms, stems removed, caps sliced
- ¼ cup soy sauce
- 4 cups beef broth
- 4 ounces (113 g) dried shiitake mushrooms, crumbled

1. Lightly coat the inside of a 5- to 7-quart Ninja Foodi PossibleCooker with nonstick cooking spray, then add the bulgur. In a large skillet over medium-high heat, warm the oil. Add the chopped onion, minced garlic, and sliced fresh mushrooms, sautéing until the onion becomes translucent and any liquid from the mushrooms has evaporated. Remove the skillet from heat, pour in the soy sauce, and scrape up any browned bits from the bottom of the pan.2. Transfer the mixture from the skillet into the Ninja Foodi PossibleCooker, and stir in the broth and dried mushrooms.

Cover and cook on low for 5 to 6 hours, or until the bulgur is tender and the broth has been fully absorbed.3. Keep the Ninja Foodi PossibleCooker on the warm setting and serve directly from it.

Savory Wild Rice Pilaf

Prep time: 10 minutes | Cook time: 3½ to 5 hours | Serves 6

- 1½ cups wild rice, uncooked
- ½ cup finely chopped onion
- 1 (14-ounce / 397-g) chicken broth
- 2 cups water
- 1 (4-ounce / 113-g) can sliced mushrooms, drained
- ½ teaspoon dried thyme leaves
- Nonstick cooking spray

1. Spray Ninja Foodi PossibleCooker with nonstick cooking spray. 2. Rinse rice and drain well. 3. Combine rice, onion, chicken broth, and water in Ninja Foodi PossibleCooker. Mix well. 4. Cover and cook on high 3 to 4 hours. 5. Add mushrooms and thyme and stir gently. 6. Cover and cook on low 30 to 60 minutes longer, or until wild rice pops and is tender.

Kidney Beans

Prep time: 15 minutes | Cook time: 6 to 7 hours | Serves 12

- 2 (30-ounce / 850-g) cans kidney beans, rinsed and drained
- 1 (28-ounce / 794-g) can diced tomatoes, drained
- 2 medium red bell peppers, chopped
- 1 cup ketchup
- ½ cup brown sugar
- ¼ cup honey
- ¼ cup molasses
- 1 tablespoon Worcestershire sauce
- 1 teaspoon dry mustard
- 2 medium red apples, cored, cut into pieces

1. Place all the ingredients, except for the apples, into the Ninja Foodi PossibleCooker and mix well to combine.2. Cover the Ninja Foodi PossibleCooker with the lid and cook on low heat for 4 to 5 hours.3. Add the apples, stirring them into the mixture.4. Cover again and continue cooking for an additional 2 hours, or until the apples are tender and the flavors are melded.

Bacon-Beef Calico Bean Bake

Prep time: 20 minutes | Cook time: 2 to 6 hours | Serves 10

- ¼ to ½ pound (227 g) bacon
- 1 pound (454 g) ground beef
- 1 medium onion, chopped
- 1 (2-pound / 907-g) can pork and beans
- 1 (1-pound / 454-g) can Great Northern beans, drained
- 1 (14½-ounce / 411-g) can
- French-style green beans, drained
- ½ cup brown sugar
- ½ cup ketchup
- ½ teaspoon salt
- 2 tablespoons cider vinegar
- 1 tablespoon prepared mustard

1. Brown bacon, ground beef, and onion in skillet until soft. Drain. 2. Combine all ingredients in Ninja Foodi PossibleCooker. 3. Cover Cook on low 5 to 6 hours, or on high 2 to 3 hours.

Auntie Ginny's Baked Beans

Prep time: 15 minutes | Cook time: 4 to 5 hours | Serves 8

- 4 slices bacon, diced
- 1 (28-ounce / 794-g) can pork and beans
- 1 teaspoon dark molasses
- 1 tablespoon brown sugar
- 1 cup dates, cut up
- 1 medium onion, chopped

1. Partially cook the bacon in a skillet until it begins to crisp but is not fully cooked. Drain off the excess grease. 2. Add all the ingredients, including the partially fried bacon, into the Ninja Foodi PossibleCooker, stirring to combine. 3. Cover and cook on low heat for 4 to 5 hours, allowing the flavors to blend and the dish to fully cook.

Meaty Slow-Cooked Jambalaya

Prep time: 25 minutes | Cook time: 7¼ hours | Serves 12

- 1 (28-ounce / 794-g) can diced tomatoes, undrained
- 1 cup reduced-sodium chicken broth
- 1 large green pepper, chopped
- 1 medium onion, chopped
- 2 celery ribs, sliced
- ½ cup white wine or additional reduced-sodium chicken broth
- 4 garlic cloves, minced
- 2 teaspoons Cajun seasoning
- 2 teaspoons dried parsley

flakes
- 1 teaspoon dried basil
- 1 teaspoon dried oregano
- ¾ teaspoon salt
- ½ to 1 teaspoon cayenne pepper
- 2 pounds (907 g) boneless skinless chicken thighs, cut into 1-inch pieces
- 1 (12-ounce / 340-g) package fully cooked andouille or other spicy chicken sausage links
- 2 pounds (907 g) uncooked medium shrimp, peeled and deveined
- 8 cups hot cooked brown rice

1. In a large bowl, mix together the first 13 ingredients to create a flavorful tomato-based sauce. Place the chicken and sausage into a 6-quart Ninja Foodi PossibleCooker, then pour the tomato mixture over the top, ensuring the meat is fully coated. Cover and cook on low for 7 to 9 hours, or until the chicken is tender. 2. Add the shrimp to the Ninja Foodi PossibleCooker, stir to combine, and cover. Cook for an additional 15 to 20 minutes, or until the shrimp turn pink and are cooked through. Serve hot over rice.

Zesty Vegetarian Chili

Prep time: 35 minutes | Cook time: 6 hours | Serves 7

- 1 (16-ounce / 454-g) can kidney beans, rinsed and drained
- 1 (15-ounce / 425-g) can black beans, rinsed and drained
- 1 (14½-ounce / 411-g) can diced tomatoes, undrained
- 1½ cups frozen corn
- 1 large onion, chopped
- 1 medium zucchini, chopped
- 1 medium sweet red pepper, chopped
- 1 (4-ounce / 113-g) can chopped green chilies
- 1 ounce (28 g) Mexican
- chocolate, chopped
- 1 cup water
- 1 (6-ounce / 170-g) can tomato paste
- 1 tablespoon cornmeal
- 1 tablespoon chili powder
- ½ teaspoon salt
- ½ teaspoon dried oregano
- ½ teaspoon ground cumin
- ¼ teaspoon hot pepper sauce (optional)
- Optional toppings: diced tomatoes, chopped green onions and crumbled queso fresco

1. In a 4-quart Ninja Foodi PossibleCooker, combine the first nine ingredients. Combine the water, tomato paste, cornmeal, chili powder, salt, oregano, cumin and pepper sauce if desired until smooth; stir into Ninja Foodi PossibleCooker. Cover and cook on low for 6 to 8 hours or until vegetables are tender. 2. Serve with toppings of your choice.

Split Chickpeas with Turnips

Prep time: 10 minutes | Cook time: 4 to 7 hours | Serves 6

- 2 teaspoons cumin seeds, divided
- 1 teaspoon mustard seeds
- 1 teaspoon coriander seeds
- 1 tablespoon rapeseed oil
- 1½-inch piece cassia bark
- 4 small turnips, peeled and chopped
- 1 cup dried split chickpeas, washed
- 4 cups hot water
- 3 ripe tomatoes, chopped
- finely
- 1 or 2 fresh green chiles, chopped
- 1½-inch piece fresh ginger, grated
- 1 small onion, sliced
- 2 garlic cloves, sliced
- ½ teaspoon turmeric
- 1 teaspoon salt
- ½ teaspoon chili powder
- Handful fresh coriander leaves, chopped

1. Preheat the Ninja Foodi PossibleCooker on high to get it warm.2. In a dry frying pan, toast 1 teaspoon of cumin seeds, mustard seeds, and coriander seeds over medium heat until they darken slightly and release a fragrant aroma. Use a mortar and pestle or a spice grinder to crush the roasted spices.3. Pour the oil into the Ninja Foodi PossibleCooker and let it heat up. Add the cassia bark and the remaining cumin seeds, allowing them to sizzle for a few moments to release their flavors.4. Add the chopped turnips, split chickpeas, and water into the Ninja Foodi PossibleCooker. Stir in the tomatoes, green chiles, grated ginger, chopped onion, and minced garlic. Mix in the turmeric, salt, chili powder, and the crushed spice blend.5. Cover and cook on high for 4 hours or on low for 6 hours. If you prefer a thicker dhal, remove the lid and continue cooking on high for an additional 30 minutes to 1 hour.6. Once the dhal is soft and fully cooked, stir in the chopped coriander leaves and serve warm.

Bacon-Infused Refried Beans

Prep time: 5 minutes | Cook time: 5 hours | Serves 8

- 2 cups dried red or pinto beans
- 6 cups water
- 2 garlic cloves, minced
- 1 large tomato, peeled,
- seeded, and chopped, or 1 pint tomato juice
- 1 teaspoon salt
- ½ pound (227 g) bacon
- Shredded cheese

1. Combine beans, water, garlic, tomato, and salt in Ninja Foodi PossibleCooker. 2. Cover. Cook on high 5 hours, stirring occasionally. When the beans become soft, drain off some liquid. 3. While the beans cook, brown bacon in skillet. Drain, reserving drippings. Crumble bacon. Add half of bacon and 3 tablespoons drippings to beans. Stir. 4. Mash or purée beans with a food processor. Fry the mashed bean mixture in the remaining bacon drippings. Add more salt to taste. 5. To serve, sprinkle the remaining bacon and shredded cheese on top of beans.

Veggie Cassoulet

Prep time: 30 minutes | Cook time: 5½ to 6½ hours | Serves 8

- 2 cups Great Northern beans, soaked overnight in water to cover and drained
- ½ cup brown lentils
- ½ cup yellow split peas
- ½ cup extra-virgin olive oil
- 2 medium onions, coarsely chopped
- 5 cloves garlic, minced
- 1 teaspoon dried thyme
- Pinch of red pepper flakes
- 4 medium carrots, cut into ½-inch rounds
- 4 stalks celery, cut into ½-inch pieces
- 2 parsnips, cut into ½-inch rounds
- 1 cup red wine, such as Burgundy
- Grated zest of 1 orange
- 1 (14- to 15-ounce / 397- to 425-g) can crushed tomatoes
- 8 cups chicken or vegetable broth
- 1 bay leaf
- Salt and freshly ground black pepper
- 2 tablespoons butter, melted
- 1 cup fresh bread crumbs
- ⅓ cup grated Parmesan cheese
- ½ cup finely chopped Italian parsley

1. Place the beans, lentils, and split peas into the insert of a 5- to 7-quart Ninja Foodi PossibleCooker. Heat the oil in a large skillet over medium-high heat. Add the chopped onions, minced garlic, thyme, and red pepper flakes, and sauté until the onions are soft and fragrant.2. Transfer the sautéed mixture from the skillet into the Ninja Foodi PossibleCooker. Add the carrots, celery, parsnips, wine, lemon zest, tomatoes, broth, and bay leaf, stirring to combine. Cover and cook on high for 5 to 6 hours, or until the beans are tender. Check periodically to see if more broth is needed and add as necessary.3. Once the beans are fully cooked, remove and discard the bay leaf. Season the cassoulet with salt and pepper to taste. In a separate mixing bowl, combine the softened butter, bread crumbs, grated cheese, and chopped parsley, then sprinkle the mixture evenly over the top of the cassoulet. Cook uncovered for an additional 30 minutes to create a crispy topping.4. Keep the dish warm in the Ninja Foodi PossibleCooker and serve as a hearty vegetarian main or flavorful side dish.

BBQ Sweet Potato Black Bean Bowl

Prep time: 15 minutes | Cook time: 2 to 4 hours | Serves 4 to 6

- 4 large sweet potatoes, peeled and cut into 8 chunks each
- 1 (15-ounce / 425-g) can black beans, rinsed and
- drained
- 1 medium onion, diced
- 2 ribs celery, sliced
- 9 ounces (255 g) Sweet Baby Ray's Barbecue Sauce

1. Place sweet potatoes in Ninja Foodi PossibleCooker. 2. Combine remaining ingredients. Pour over sweet potatoes. 3. Cover. Cook on high 2 to 3 hours, or on low 4 hours.

Hearty Baked Bean Casserole

Prep time: 15 minutes | Cook time: 3 hours | Serves 6 to 8

- 1 pound (454 g) ground beef
- ½ cup chopped onions
- ½ teaspoon taco seasoning, or more
- 1 or 2 (15-ounce / 425-g) cans pork and beans
- ¾ cup barbecue sauce

1. Brown ground beef and onions in a nonstick skillet. Drain. 2. Stir all ingredients together in the Ninja Foodi PossibleCooker, including the browned ground beef and onions. 3. Cover and cook on low 3 hours.

Apple Bean Bake

Prep time: 20 minutes | Cook time: 2 to 4 hours | Serves 10 to 12

- 4 tablespoons butter
- 2 large Granny Smith apples, cubed
- ½ cup brown sugar
- ¼ cup sugar
- ½ cup ketchup
- 1 teaspoon cinnamon
- 1 tablespoon molasses
- 1 teaspoon salt
- 1 (24-ounce / 680-g) can Great Northern beans, undrained
- 1 (24-ounce / 680-g) can pinto beans, undrained
- Ham chunks (optional)

1. Melt the butter in a skillet over medium heat. Add the sliced apples and cook until they are tender and slightly caramelized.2. Stir in the brown sugar and granulated sugar, cooking until both sugars have melted and formed a syrupy consistency. Add the ketchup, cinnamon, molasses, and salt, stirring well to combine all the flavors.3. Add the beans and chunks of ham to the skillet, mixing everything thoroughly. Transfer the mixture into the Ninja Foodi PossibleCooker, spreading it out evenly.4. Cover and cook on high for 2 to 4 hours, or until the beans are heated through and the flavors have melded together.

Hearty Mixed Bean Medley

Prep time: 10 minutes | Cook time: 4 to 5 hours | Serves 6

- 1 (16-ounce / 454-g) can kidney beans, drained
- 1 (15½-ounce / 439-g) can baked beans, undrained
- 1 pint home-frozen, or 1 (1-pound / 454-g) package frozen, lima beans
- 1 pint home-frozen, or 1 (1-pound / 454-g) package
- frozen, green beans
- 4 slices lean turkey bacon, browned and crumbled
- ½ cup ketchup
- ⅓ cup sugar
- ⅓ cup brown sugar
- 2 tablespoons vinegar
- ½ teaspoon salt

1. Combine beans and bacon in Ninja Foodi PossibleCooker. 2. Stir together remaining ingredients. Add to beans and mix well. 3. Cover. Cook on low 4 to 5 hours.

Smoky BBQ Bean Bake

Prep time: 20 minutes | Cook time: 4 to 6 hours | Serves 10 to 12

- 1 large onion, chopped
- 1 pound (454 g) ground beef, browned
- 1 (15-ounce / 425-g) can pork and beans
- 1 (15-ounce / 425-g) can ranch-style beans, drained
- 1 (16-ounce / 454-g) can kidney beans, drained
- 1 cup ketchup
- 1 teaspoon salt
- 1 tablespoon prepared mustard
- 2 tablespoons brown sugar
- 2 tablespoons hickory-flavored barbecue sauce
- ½ to 1 pound (227 to 454 g) small smoky link sausages (optional)

1. Brown ground beef and onion in skillet. Drain. Transfer to Ninja Foodi PossibleCooker set on high. 2. Add remaining ingredients. Mix well. 3. Reduce heat to low and cook 4 to 6 hours. Use a paper towel to absorb oil that's risen to the top before stirring and serving.

Barbecued Baked Beans

Prep time: 10 minutes | Cook time: 3 to 4 hours | Serves 8 to 10

- 2 (16-ounce / 454-g) cans baked beans, your choice of variety
- 2 (15-ounce / 425-g) cans kidney or pinto beans, or one
- of each, drained
- ½ cup brown sugar
- 1 cup ketchup
- 1 onion, chopped

1. Add all the ingredients to the Ninja Foodi PossibleCooker and stir thoroughly to ensure everything is well mixed.2. Cover with the lid and cook on low for 3 to 4 hours, or until the dish is heated through and flavors are well combined.

Quinoa Chicken Chili

Prep time: 30 minutes | Cook time: 5 to 7 hours | Serves 8

- 1 teaspoon olive oil
- ½ yellow onion, minced
- 2 cloves garlic, minced
- 2 large boneless, skinless chicken breasts, diced
- 1 cup quinoa, rinsed
- 1 (28-ounce / 794-g) can crushed tomatoes, with the juice
- 1 (15-ounce / 425-g) can diced tomatoes with green chiles, with the juice
- 2 (15-ounce / 425-g) cans black beans, drained and rinsed
- 2 pounds (907 g) corn
- kernels, fresh or frozen and thawed
- 1 large bell pepper, any color, chopped
- 2½ cups chicken stock
- 1 teaspoon ground cumin
- 1 teaspoon red pepper flakes
- 1 teaspoon chili powder
- ½ teaspoon sea salt
- ½ teaspoon black pepper
- 1 (8-ounce / 227-g) container of plain Greek yogurt, for serving (optional)
- ½ cup grated Parmesan cheese, for serving (optional)

1. Warm the olive oil in a medium skillet over medium-high heat. Add the diced onion and minced garlic, sautéing for about 1 minute until fragrant.2. Place the chicken in the skillet and cook until it is browned on all sides, roughly 5 minutes. Transfer the browned chicken to the Ninja Foodi PossibleCooker (see Note for additional instructions).3. Add the quinoa, crushed tomatoes, diced tomatoes with chiles, black beans, corn, diced bell pepper, and chicken stock to the Ninja Foodi PossibleCooker. Sprinkle in the cumin, red pepper flakes, chili powder, ½ teaspoon salt, and ½ teaspoon black pepper, stirring to combine all ingredients.4. Cover and cook on low heat for 5 to 7 hours. Once cooked, remove the chicken from the Ninja Foodi PossibleCooker, shred it with two forks, and return

the shredded chicken to the pot. Taste and adjust the seasoning with more salt and pepper if needed. Keep warm until ready to serve.5. To serve, top with Greek yogurt and/or a sprinkle of Parmesan cheese, if desired.

Full Meal Deal Beans

Prep time: 25 minutes | Cook time: 8 hours | Serves 10 to 12

- 3 cups dry pinto beans, sorted and washed
- 3 quarts water
- 1 ham bone with lots of ham still hanging on!
- 1 bunch green onions, chopped
- 1 tablespoon ground cumin (optional)
- 5½ cups water
- 1 (10¾-ounce / 305-g) can Rotel chili and tomatoes
- Salt to taste (optional)

1. Place the dry beans in a large soup kettle and cover them with 3 quarts of water. Cover and let them soak overnight or for 8 hours. For a quicker method, bring the beans and water to a boil, cook for 2 minutes, then keep covered, remove from heat, and let them stand for 1 hour. Drain the beans when ready.2. In the bottom of the Ninja Foodi PossibleCooker, place the ham bone, chopped green onions, and cumin.3. Add the drained beans over the ham bone and seasonings. Pour in 5½ cups of fresh water and add the tomatoes.4. Cover the Ninja Foodi PossibleCooker and set to high. Cook for 7 to 8 hours, or until the beans are tender and fully cooked.5. If desired, stir in salt to taste and let the dish stand for 15 minutes before serving to allow the flavors to meld.

Savory Wild Rice Medley

Prep time: 10 minutes | Cook time: 2½ to 3 hours | Serves 5

- 1 cup wild rice or wild rice mixture, uncooked
- ½ cup sliced fresh mushrooms
- ½ cup diced onions
- ½ cup diced green or red bell
- peppers
- 1 tablespoon oil
- ½ teaspoon salt
- ¼ teaspoon black pepper
- 2½ cups fat-free, low-sodium chicken broth

1. Layer rice and vegetables in Ninja Foodi PossibleCooker. Pour oil, salt, and pepper over vegetables. Stir. 2. Heat chicken broth. Pour over all ingredients in Ninja Foodi PossibleCooker. 3. Cover. Cook on high 2½ to 3 hours, or until rice is soft and liquid is absorbed.

Chapter 3

Beef, Pork, and Lamb

Chapter 3 Beef, Pork, and Lamb

BBQ Burgers

Prep time: 20 minutes | Cook time: 3 to 6 hours | Makes 4 sandwiches

- 1 pound (454 g) ground beef
- ¼ cup chopped onions
- 3 tablespoons ketchup
- 1 teaspoon salt
- 1 egg, beaten
- ¼ cup seasoned bread crumbs
- 1 (18-ounce / 510-g) bottle of your favorite barbecue sauce

1. Combine beef, onions, ketchup, salt, egg, and bread crumbs. Form into 4 patties. Brown both sides lightly in skillet. Place in Ninja Foodi PossibleCooker. 2. Cover with barbecue sauce. 3. Cover. Cook on high 3 hours, or on low 6 hours.

Three-Bean Burrito Bake

Prep time: 30 minutes | Cook time: 8 to 10 hours | Serves 6

- 1 tablespoon oil
- 1 onion, chopped
- 1 green bell pepper, chopped
- 2 garlic cloves, minced
- 1 (16-ounce / 454-g) can pinto beans, drained
- 1 (16-ounce / 454-g) can kidney beans, drained
- 1 (15-ounce / 425-g) can black beans, drained
- 1 (4-ounce / 113-g) can
- sliced black olives, drained
- 1 (4-ounce / 113-g) can green chilies
- 2 (15-ounce / 425-g) cans diced tomatoes
- 1 teaspoon chili powder
- 1 teaspoon ground cumin
- 6 to 8 (6-inch) flour tortillas
- 2 cups shredded Co-Jack cheese
- Sour cream

1. Heat the oil in a large skillet over medium heat and sauté the chopped onions, green peppers, and minced garlic until softened and fragrant.2. Stir in the beans, sliced olives, chilies, diced tomatoes, chili powder, and cumin, mixing well to combine all the flavors.3. In a greased Ninja Foodi PossibleCooker, layer ¾ cup of the vegetable mixture, followed by a tortilla and then ⅓ cup of shredded cheese. Repeat the layers until all the ingredients are used, finishing with the remaining vegetable mixture on top.4. Cover and cook on low for 8 to 10 hours, allowing the flavors to meld and

the dish to set.5. Serve hot, topped with dollops of sour cream on individual servings for a creamy finish.

Cola-Infused Beef Roast

Prep time: 15 minutes | Cook time: 5 to 10 hours | Serves 6 to 8

- 3 to 4 pounds (1.4 to 1.8 kg) beef roast
- 1 (12-ounce / 340-g) can cola
- 1 (10¾-ounce / 305-g) can cream of mushroom soup
- 1 envelope dry onion soup mix

1. Place beef in Ninja Foodi PossibleCooker. 2. In a small bowl, blend cola and mushroom soup together. Pour over roast. 3. Sprinkle with dry onion soup mix. 4. Cover and cook on low for 10 hours, or on high for 5 hours, or until meat is tender but not dry.

Stuffed Bell Peppers

Prep time: 25 minutes | Cook time: 6 hours | Serves 4

- 3 tablespoons extra-virgin olive oil, divided
- 1 pound (454 g) ground beef
- ½ cup finely chopped cauliflower
- 1 tomato, diced
- ½ sweet onion, chopped
- 2 teaspoons minced garlic
- 2 teaspoons dried oregano
- 1 teaspoon dried basil
- 4 bell peppers, tops cut off and seeded
- 1 cup shredded Cheddar cheese
- ½ cup chicken broth
- 1 tablespoon basil, sliced into thin strips, for garnish

1. Lightly grease the insert of the Ninja Foodi PossibleCooker with 1 tablespoon of the olive oil. 2. In a large skillet over medium-high heat, heat the remaining 2 tablespoons of the olive oil. Add the beef and sauté until it is cooked through, about 10 minutes. 3. Add the cauliflower, tomato, onion, garlic, oregano, and basil. Sauté for an additional 5 minutes. 4. Spoon the meat mixture into the bell peppers and top with the cheese. 5. Place the peppers in the Ninja Foodi PossibleCooker and add the broth to the bottom. 6. Cover and cook on low for 6 hours. 7. Serve warm, topped with the basil.

Tiajuana Tacos

Prep time: 20 minutes | Cook time: 2 hours | Serves 6

- 3 cups cooked chopped beef
- 1 (1-pound / 454-g) can refried beans
- ½ cup chopped onions
- ½ cup chopped green peppers
- ½ cup chopped ripe olives
- 1 (8-ounce / 227-g) can tomato sauce
- 3 teaspoons chili powder
- 1 tablespoon Worcestershire sauce
- ½ teaspoon garlic powder
- ¼ teaspoon pepper
- ¼ teaspoon paprika
- ⅛ teaspoon celery salt
- ⅛ teaspoon ground nutmeg
- ¾ cup water
- 1 teaspoon salt
- 1 cup crushed corn chips
- 6 taco shells
- Shredded lettuce
- Chopped tomatoes
- Shredded Cheddar cheese

1. Add the first 15 ingredients to the Ninja Foodi PossibleCooker, stirring well to combine everything evenly. 2. Cover the Ninja Foodi PossibleCooker and set it to cook on high for 2 hours, allowing the flavors to blend and the ingredients to cook through. 3. Right before serving, gently fold in the corn chips to add a crunchy texture. 4. Spoon the mixture into taco shells and top with fresh lettuce, diced tomatoes, and shredded cheese for a delicious meal.

Honey Teriyaki Pork Roast

Prep time: 15 minutes | Cook time: 7 hours | Serves 2

- 1½ pounds (680 g) boneless pork roast
- 2 garlic cloves, cut into slivers
- ¼ cup honey
- 1 onion, sliced
- ¼ cup orange juice
- 2 tablespoons low-sodium soy sauce
- 1 tablespoon teriyaki sauce
- 3 tablespoons brown sugar
- 2 teaspoons grated fresh ginger
- ⅛ teaspoon freshly ground black pepper
- 2 tablespoons water
- 1 tablespoon cornstarch

1. Using a sharp knife, poke about a dozen holes in the pork roast. Insert the garlic slivers into the holes. Drizzle the roast with the honey and rub it in. 2. In the Ninja Foodi PossibleCooker, put the roast on top of the onion. 3. In a small bowl, mix the orange juice, soy sauce, teriyaki sauce, sugar, ginger, and pepper and pour the mixture over the roast. 4. Cover and cook on low for 6 to 7 hours, or until the roast is very tender. Remove the roast and onion from the Ninja Foodi PossibleCooker to a platter and cover. 5. In a small bowl, mix the water and cornstarch well. Stir the mixture into the liquid in the Ninja Foodi PossibleCooker and turn the heat to high. Cook for 10 to 15 minutes, until thickened. 6. Serve the sauce with the pork and onion.

Beef Ribs

Prep time: 5 minutes | Cook time: 8½ hours | Serves 8 to 10

- 1 (3- to 4-pound / 1.4- to 1.8-kg) boneless beef or short ribs
- 1½ cups barbecue sauce, divided
- ½ cup apricot or pineapple jam
- 1 tablespoon soy sauce

1. Arrange the ribs in a baking dish. 2. In a bowl, mix ¾ cup of barbecue sauce with the jam and soy sauce until well combined. Drizzle this mixture over the ribs and bake at 450°F (235°C) for 30 minutes, or until the ribs are nicely browned. 3. Remove from the oven, then transfer the ribs and their juices into a Ninja Foodi PossibleCooker. 4. Cover and set the Ninja Foodi PossibleCooker to low, allowing the ribs to cook for 8 hours until they are tender. 5. Combine the remaining ¾ cup of barbecue sauce with the juices from the Ninja Foodi PossibleCooker, stirring well. Coat the ribs with this sauce before serving.

Applesauce-Glazed Meatballs

Prep time: 40 minutes | Cook time: 4 to 6 hours | Serves 6

- ¾ pound (340 g) ground beef
- ¼ pound (113 g) ground pork
- 1 egg
- ¾ cup soft bread crumbs
- ½ cup unsweetened applesauce
- ¾ teaspoon salt
- ¼ teaspoon pepper
- Oil
- ¼ cup ketchup
- ¼ cup water

1. Combine beef, pork, egg, bread crumbs, applesauce, salt, and pepper. Form into 1½-inch balls. 2. Brown in oil in batches in skillet. 3. Transfer meat to Ninja Foodi PossibleCooker, reserving drippings. Combine ketchup and water and pour into skillet. Stir up browned drippings and mix well. Spoon over meatballs. 4. Cover. Cook on low 4 to 6 hours. 5. Serve.

Cheesy Beef Macaroni

Prep time: 20 minutes | Cook time: 2 to 2½ hours | Serves 4 to 5

- 1 pound (454 g) ground beef
- 1 small onion, chopped
- Half a green pepper, chopped
- 1 cup macaroni, cooked
- ½ teaspoon dried basil
- ½ teaspoon dried thyme
- 1 teaspoon Worcestershire sauce
- 1 teaspoon salt
- 1 (10¾-ounce / 305-g) can Cheddar cheese soup

1. Brown beef, onions, and green pepper in skillet. Pour off drippings and place meat and vegetables in Ninja Foodi PossibleCooker. 2. Combine all ingredients in cooker. 3. Cover. Cook on high 2 to 2½ hours, stirring once or twice. 4. Serve.

Chinese Hamburger

Prep time: 15 minutes | Cook time: 3 to 4 hours | Serves 8

- 1 pound (454 g) ground beef, browned and drained
- 1 onion, diced
- 2 ribs celery, diced
- 1 (10¾-ounce / 305-g) can chicken noodle soup
- 1 (10¾-ounce / 305-g) can cream of mushroom soup
- 1 (12-ounce / 340-g) can Chinese vegetables
- Salt to taste, about ¼ to ½ teaspoon
- Pepper to taste, about ¼ teaspoon
- 1 green pepper, diced
- 1 teaspoon soy sauce

1. Place all the ingredients into the Ninja Foodi PossibleCooker, ensuring they are well mixed. 2. Cover and cook on high for 3 to 4 hours, stirring occasionally if needed. 3. Serve hot and enjoy.

Creamy Slow-Cooked Pork Chops

Prep time: 10 minutes | Cook time: 4 to 5 hours | Serves 6

- 1 (10¾-ounce / 305-g) can 98% fat-free cream of chicken soup
- 1 onion, chopped
- 3 tablespoons ketchup
- 2 teaspoons Worcestershire sauce
- 6 whole pork chops, boneless or bone-in, divided

1. Mix soup and chopped onions together in a bowl. Stir in ketchup and Worcestershire sauce. Pour half of mixture into Ninja Foodi PossibleCooker. 2. Place pork chops in Ninja Foodi PossibleCooker. If you have to stack them, spoon a proportionate amount of the remaining sauce over the first layer of meat. 3. Add the rest of the chops. Cover with the remaining sauce. 4. Cover and cook on low 4 to 5 hours, or until meat is tender but not dry.

Beef Enchiladas

Prep time: 15 minutes | Cook time: 4 to 5 hours | Serves 12 to 16

- 1 (4-pound / 1.8-kg) boneless chuck roast
- 2 tablespoons oil
- 4 cups sliced onions
- 2 teaspoons salt
- 2 teaspoons black pepper
- 2 teaspoons cumin seeds
- 2 (4½-ounce / 128-g) cans
- peeled, diced green chilies
- 1 (14½-ounce / 411-g) can peeled, diced tomatoes
- 8 large tortillas (10 to 12 inch size)
- 1 pound (454 g) Cheddar cheese, shredded
- 4 cups green or red enchilada sauce

1. In a saucepan, heat oil and brown the roast on all sides. Transfer the roast to the Ninja Foodi PossibleCooker. 2. Add all the remaining ingredients to the Ninja Foodi PossibleCooker, except for the tortillas, cheese, and enchilada sauce. 3. Cover and cook on high for 4 to 5 hours. 4. Use a fork to shred the meat, then return it to the Ninja Foodi PossibleCooker and mix well. 5. Warm the tortillas in the oven and heat the enchilada sauce. Fill each tortilla with ¾ cup of the beef mixture and ½ cup of cheese. Roll them up and serve drizzled with the enchilada sauce.

Pecos River Red-Frito Pie

Prep time: 10 minutes | Cook time: 8 to 10 hours | Serves 6

- 1 large onion, chopped coarsely
- 3 pounds (1.4 kg) coarsely ground hamburger
- 2 garlic cloves, minced
- 3 tablespoons ground hot red chili peppers
- 2 tablespoons ground mild red chili peppers
- 1½ cups water
- Corn chips
- Shredded Monterey Jack cheese
- Shredded Cheddar cheese

1. Place the onion, ground beef, garlic, chilies, and water into the Ninja Foodi PossibleCooker. 2. Cover and cook on low for 8 to 10 hours, then drain any excess liquid. 3. Spoon the mixture over corn chips and garnish with a blend of Monterey Jack and Cheddar cheeses.

Classic Corned Beef and Vegetables

Prep time: 10 minutes | Cook time: 10 to 11 hours | Serves 6

- 2 onions, sliced
- 2 garlic cloves, minced
- 3 potatoes, pared and quartered
- 3 carrots, sliced
- 2 bay leaves
- 1 small head cabbage, cut into 4 wedges
- 1 (3- to 4-pound / 1.4- to 1.8-kg) corned beef brisket
- 1 cup water
- ½ cup brown sugar
- 1 tablespoon prepared mustard
- Dash of ground cloves

1. Layer onions, garlic, potatoes, carrots, bay leaves, and cabbage in Ninja Foodi PossibleCooker. 2. Place brisket on top. 3. Add water. 4. Cover. Cook on low 10 to 11 hours. 5. During last hour of cooking, combine brown sugar, mustard, and cloves. Spread over beef. 6. Discard bay leaves. Slice meat and arrange on platter of vegetables.

Easy Meatballs for a Group

Prep time: 5 minutes | Cook time: 4 hours | Serves 10 to 12

- 80 to 100 frozen small meatballs
- 1 (16-ounce / 454-g) jar
- barbecue sauce
- 1 (16-ounce / 454-g) jar apricot jam

1. Place the meatballs into the Ninja Foodi PossibleCooker, filling it evenly. 2. In a separate bowl, mix together the sauce and jam until smooth. Pour the mixture over the meatballs, ensuring they are well coated. 3. Cover the Ninja Foodi PossibleCooker and cook on low for 4 hours, stirring occasionally to make sure the meatballs are evenly heated and coated with sauce. 4. Serve warm, either as an appetizer or as a main dish, depending on your preference.

Pigs in Blankets

Prep time: 30 minutes | Cook time: 6 to 8 hours | Serves 4

- 1 (1- to 2-pound / 454 to 907-g) round steak
- 1 pound (454 g) bacon
- 1 cup ketchup
- ¼ cup brown sugar
- 1 small onion
- ¼ to ½ cup water

1. Slice the round steak into long strips and roll each strip into a spiral. Wrap a slice of bacon around each rolled steak piece, securing it with a toothpick. 2. Heat the remaining ingredients in a saucepan over medium heat until they simmer, forming a flavorful sauce. 3. Arrange the meat rolls in the Ninja Foodi PossibleCooker and pour the prepared sauce evenly over them. 4. Cover and cook on low for 6 to 8 hours, until the meat is tender but still holds its shape.

Hearty Beef and Veggie Casserole

Prep time: 20 minutes | Cook time: 4 to 5 hours | Serves 8

- 1 pound (454 g) extra-lean ground beef or turkey
- 1 medium onion, chopped
- ½ cup chopped celery
- 4 cups chopped cabbage
- 2½ cups canned stewed tomatoes, slightly mashed
- 1 tablespoon flour
- 1 teaspoon salt
- 1 tablespoon sugar
- ¼ to ½ teaspoon black pepper, according to your taste preference

1. Sauté meat, onion, and celery in nonstick skillet until meat is browned. 2. Pour into Ninja Foodi PossibleCooker. 3. Top with layers of cabbage, tomatoes, flour, salt, sugar, and pepper. 4. Cover. Cook on high 4 to 5 hours.

Barbecued Spoonburgers

Prep time: 15 minutes | Cook time: 3 to 8 hours | Serves 6 to 8

- 2 tablespoons oil
- 1½ pounds (680 g) ground beef
- ½ cup chopped onions
- ½ cup diced celery
- Half a green pepper, chopped
- 1 tablespoon Worcestershire sauce
- ½ cup ketchup
- 1 garlic clove, minced
- 1 teaspoon salt
- ¾ cup water
- ⅛ teaspoon pepper
- ½ teaspoon paprika
- 1 (6-ounce / 170-g) can tomato paste
- 2 tablespoons vinegar
- 2 teaspoons brown sugar
- 1 teaspoon dry mustard

1. Heat oil in a saucepan and brown the beef until fully seared. Drain any excess fat. 2. Transfer the browned beef and all other ingredients into the Ninja Foodi PossibleCooker, mixing well. 3. Cover and cook on low for 6 to 8 hours, or on high for 3 to 4 hours, until the flavors are well combined. 4. Serve hot and enjoy.

Dilled Pot Roast with Creamy Sauce

Prep time: 5 minutes | Cook time: 7¼ to 9¼ hours | Serves 8

- 1 (2¾-pound / 1.3-kg) beef pot roast
- 1 teaspoon salt
- ¼ teaspoon black pepper
- 2 teaspoons dried dill weed, divided
- ¼ cup water
- 2 tablespoons wine vinegar
- 4 tablespoons flour
- ½ cup water
- 2 cups fat-free sour cream

1. Sprinkle both sides of beef with salt, pepper, and 1 teaspoon dill weed. Place in Ninja Foodi PossibleCooker. 2. Add ¼ cup water and vinegar. 3. Cover. Cook on low 7 to 9 hours. 4. Remove meat from pot. Turn cooker to high. 5. Stir flour into ½ cup water. Stir into meat drippings. 6. Stir in additional 1 teaspoon dill weed if you wish. 7. Cover. Cook on high 5 minutes. 8. Stir in sour cream. 9. Cover. Cook on high another 5 minutes. 10. Slice beef and serve.

Osso Bucco-Style Pork Tenderloin

Prep time: 30 minutes | Cook time: 6 hours | Serves 10

- 2 tablespoons unsalted butter
- 1 tablespoon olive oil
- 4 pounds (1.8 kg) pork tenderloin, silver skin removed, cut into 1-inch cubes
- 1½ teaspoons salt
- 1 teaspoon freshly ground black pepper
- 1 cup finely chopped onion
- 1 cup finely chopped carrots
- 1 cup finely chopped celery
- 1 teaspoon dried sage
- ½ cup dry white wine or vermouth
- ½ cup chicken broth
- ½ cup beef broth
- 1 (15-ounce / 425-g) can chopped plum tomatoes, with their juice
- 4 cloves garlic, minced
- Grated zest of 1 lemon
- Grated zest of 1 orange
- ½ cup finely chopped fresh parsley

1. Heat the butter and oil in a large skillet over medium-high heat. Sprinkle the pork with the salt and pepper. Add to the skillet in several batches and brown until nicely crusted on all sides. 2. Transfer the pork to the insert of a 5- to 7-quart Ninja Foodi PossibleCooker. Add the onion, carrots, celery, and sage to the same skillet and cook, stirring, until the onion begins to soften and turn translucent, about 5 minutes. 3. Add the wine and scrape up any browned bits from the bottom of the pan. Transfer to the slow-cooker insert. Add both broths and the tomatoes and stir to combine. Cover and cook on low for 6 hours, until the meat is fork tender. 4. Skim off any fat from the top of the sauce. Stir in the garlic, lemon and orange zests, and parsley. 5. Serve from the cooker set on warm.

Red Wine–Marinated Sirloin

Prep time: 20 minutes | Cook time: 3¼ hours | Serves 8

- 4 cups Burgundy wine
- 3 cloves garlic, minced
- 1 teaspoon dried thyme
- 1 bay leaf
- 2 tablespoons honey
- 1 teaspoon salt
- ½ teaspoon freshly ground black pepper
- 3 to 4 pounds (1.4 to 1.8 kg) beef sirloin, fat trimmed, cut into 1-inch pieces
- 6 strips thick-cut bacon, cut into ½-inch pieces
- 1 (15-ounce / 425-g) can double-strength beef broth
- 4 tablespoons (½ stick) unsalted butter, at room temperature
- 1 pound (454 g) small white button mushrooms
- ½ pound (227 g) pearl onions, blanched and peeled
- 3 tablespoons all-purpose flour

1. In a large zipper-top plastic bag, mix together the wine, garlic, thyme, bay leaf, honey, salt, and pepper. Add the beef, seal the bag, and shake to coat the meat thoroughly. Refrigerate for at least 8 hours, or up to 24 hours, turning the bag occasionally. 2. Remove the beef from the marinade and set the marinade aside, discarding the bay leaf. In a large skillet, cook the bacon until crispy, then transfer it to paper towels to drain. In the same skillet, brown the beef on all sides in the bacon drippings. Once browned, move the meat to the insert of a 5- to 7-quart Ninja Foodi PossibleCooker. Pour the marinade into the skillet, bringing it to a boil while scraping any browned bits from the pan. 3. Pour the contents of the skillet over the meat in the Ninja Foodi PossibleCooker, then add the broth. Cover and cook on high for 3 hours, or until the meat is tender. Meanwhile, melt 2 tablespoons of butter in a skillet over medium-high heat. Add the mushrooms and onions, sautéing until golden and the liquid evaporates. Set aside until ready to use. (These can be refrigerated for up to 2 days.) Combine the remaining 2 tablespoons of butter with flour in a bowl to create a paste. 4. After the stew has finished cooking, skim off any excess fat from the sauce. Stir in the butter and flour mixture, then add the mushroom and onion mixture along with the reserved bacon. Mix well and cover, cooking for an additional 15 to 20 minutes, until the sauce has thickened before serving.

Mexican Casserole

Prep time: 15 minutes | Cook time: 8 to 9 hours | Serves 8

- 1 pound (454 g) extra-lean ground beef
- 1 medium onion, chopped
- 1 small green bell pepper, chopped
- 1 (16-ounce / 454-g) can kidney beans, rinsed and drained
- 1 (14½-ounce / 411-g) can diced tomatoes, undrained
- 1 (8-ounce / 227-g) can tomato sauce
- ¼ cup water
- 1 envelope reduced-sodium taco seasoning
- 1 tablespoon chili powder
- 1⅓ cups instant rice, uncooked
- 1 cup low-fat Cheddar cheese

1. In a nonstick skillet, brown the ground beef and onion until the meat is fully cooked and the onion is softened. 2. Transfer the beef mixture to the Ninja Foodi PossibleCooker, adding all other ingredients except for the rice and cheese. 3. Cover and cook on low for 8 to 9 hours. 4. Stir in the rice, cover, and continue cooking until the rice is tender. 5. Sprinkle cheese over the top, cover, and cook until the cheese has melted. Serve warm.

Curried Meatballs

Prep time: 40 minutes | Cook time: 4 hours | Serves 8

Sauce:
- 2 tablespoons vegetable oil
- 4 cloves garlic, minced
- 2 large onions, coarsely chopped
- 2 teaspoon freshly grated ginger

Meat Balls:
- 1 pound (454 g) 85% lean ground beef
- 1 teaspoon salt
- ¼ teaspoon ground cumin
- ¼ teaspoon garam masala
- ½ teaspoon ground cumin
- 1 teaspoon sweet paprika
- Pinch of cayenne pepper
- ¼ teaspoon ground cinnamon
- 2 (32-ounce / 907-g) cans tomato purée
- ¼ cup finely minced fresh cilantro
- ½ cup nonfat yogurt
- Vegetable oil for frying (optional)

1. Warm the oil in a sauté pan over medium-high heat. Add the garlic, onions, ginger, cumin, paprika, cayenne, and cinnamon, and cook until the onions become soft, about 4 to 5 minutes. 2. Move the sautéed mixture into the insert of a 5- to 7-quart Ninja Foodi PossibleCooker. Stir in the tomato purée, cover, and set to cook on high while preparing the meatballs. 3. In a large bowl, combine all the meatball ingredients. Using clean hands or a wooden spoon, gently mix the ingredients together, being careful not to compact the mixture. Use a scoop to shape the mixture into 2-inch balls. 4. Gently place the meatballs into the sauce in the Ninja Foodi PossibleCooker. Cook on high for 1 hour, then lower the heat to low and continue cooking for 3 hours, or until an instant-read thermometer inserted into the meatballs reads 165°F (74°C). If preferred, for a crispier texture, heat ½ inch of oil in a large skillet over medium-high heat. Brown the meatballs on all sides, turning them as they develop a crust, then transfer to the Ninja Foodi PossibleCooker and proceed as directed. 5. Serve the meatballs warm from the Ninja Foodi PossibleCooker, using 6-inch skewers for easy serving.

Tangy Beef Ribs and Sauerkraut

Prep time: 10 minutes | Cook time: 3 to 8 hours | Serves 8 to 10

- 4 pounds (1.8 kg) beef short ribs
- 1 (32-ounce / 907-g) bag
- sauerkraut, drained
- 2 tablespoons caraway seeds
- ¼ cup water

1. Put ribs in 6-quart Ninja Foodi PossibleCooker. 2. Place sauerkraut and caraway seeds on top of ribs. 3. Pour in water. 4. Cover. Cook on high 3 to 4 hours, or on low 7 to 8 hours. 5. Serve.

Guinness-Braised Corned Beef

Prep time: 15 minutes | Cook time: 8 to 10 hours | Serves 6 to 8

- 2 (12-ounce / 340-g) cans Guinness or other stout or dark ale
- ¼ cup firmly packed light brown sugar
- 2 teaspoons mustard seeds
- 6 whole black peppercorns
- 1 bay leaf
- 2 allspice berries
- 3 large sweet onions, such as Vidalia, sliced into ½-inch-thick half rounds
- 1 (3½- to 4-pound / 1.6- to 1.8-kg) corned beef, rinsed

1. Stir the Guinness, sugar, mustard seeds, peppercorns, bay leaf, and allspice berries together in the insert of a 5- to 7-quart Ninja Foodi PossibleCooker. Add the onions and top with the corned beef. (Cut it in half to fit, if necessary.) 2. Cover and cook on low for 8 to 10 hours, until the meat is fork tender. Remove the meat from the cooker, cover with aluminum foil, and allow to rest for 20 minutes. 3. Remove the bay leaf, peppercorns, and allspice berries from the cooking liquid. Thinly slice the brisket across the grain to serve.

Golden Peach Pork Chops

Prep time: 5 minutes | Cook time: 3 to 4 hours | Serves 5 to 6

- 5 to 6 pork chops
- Salt to taste
- Pepper to taste
- 1 (29-ounce / 822-g) can cling peach halves, drained (reserve juice)
- ¼ cup brown sugar
- ½ teaspoon ground cinnamon
- ¼ teaspoon ground cloves
- 1 (8-ounce / 227-g) can tomato sauce
- ¼ cup vinegar

1. Lightly brown pork chops on both sides in saucepan. Drain. Arrange in Ninja Foodi PossibleCooker. Sprinkle with salt and pepper. 2. Place drained peach halves on top of pork chops. 3. Combine brown sugar, cinnamon, cloves, tomato sauce, ¼ cup peach syrup, and vinegar. Pour over peaches and pork chops. 4. Cover. Cook on low 3 to 4 hours.

Hot Italian Short Ribs

Prep time: 20 minutes | Cook time: 3½ to 8 hours | Serves 4 to 6

- 4½ pounds (2 kg) boneless short ribs, fat trimmed
- 2 teaspoons salt
- 1 teaspoon freshly ground black pepper
- 2 tablespoons extra-virgin olive oil
- 2 cups coarsely chopped sweet onion, such as Vidalia
- 6 cloves garlic, minced
- 2 medium red bell peppers, seeded and thinly sliced
- 4 hot pickled Italian peppers, drained, stems removed, and excess seeds removed
- 1 cup red wine
- 1 cup beef broth

1. Season the short ribs generously with salt and pepper. In a large skillet, heat oil over high heat and brown the beef in batches, making sure to sear all sides. 2. Once browned, transfer the meat to the insert of a 5- to 7-quart Ninja Foodi PossibleCooker. In the same skillet, add the onion, garlic, and bell peppers, sautéing until the onion and peppers are tender, about 4 minutes. 3. Stir in the pickled peppers, wine, and broth, scraping the bottom of the pan to release any browned bits. Pour this mixture into the Ninja Foodi PossibleCooker over the meat. 4. Cover and cook on high for 3½ to 4 hours, or on low for 8 hours. After cooking, remove the meat and cover it with aluminum foil to rest for 10 to 15 minutes. Skim off any fat from the sauce. 5. Serve the short ribs topped with the sautéed vegetables and sauce, with any remaining sauce on the side for extra flavor.

Italian Spaghetti Sauce

Prep time: 20 minutes | Cook time: 8 to 9 hours | Serves 8 to 10

- 2 pounds (907 g) sausage or ground beef
- 3 medium onions, chopped (about 2¼ cups)
- 2 cups sliced mushrooms
- 6 garlic cloves, minced
- 2 (14½-ounce / 411-g) cans diced tomatoes, undrained
- 1 (29-ounce / 822-g) can tomato sauce
- 1 (12-ounce / 340-g) can tomato paste
- 2 tablespoons dried basil
- 1 tablespoon dried oregano
- 1 tablespoon sugar
- 1 teaspoon salt
- ½ teaspoon crushed red pepper flakes

1. Cook sausage, onions, mushrooms, and garlic in skillet over medium heat for 10 minutes. Drain. Transfer to Ninja Foodi PossibleCooker. 2. Stir in remaining ingredients. 3. Cover. Cook on low 8 to 9 hours.

Meatball-Barley Casserole

Prep time: 40 minutes | Cook time: 4 to 8 hours | Serves 6

- ⅔ cup pearl barley
- 1 pound (454 g) ground beef
- ½ cup soft bread crumbs
- 1 small onion, chopped
- ¼ cup milk
- ¼ teaspoon pepper
- 1 teaspoon salt
- Oil
- ½ cup thinly sliced celery
- ½ cup finely chopped sweet peppers
- 1 (10¾-ounce / 305-g) can cream of celery soup
- ⅓ cup water
- Paprika

1. Prepare the barley according to the package instructions and set aside. 2. In a bowl, mix together the beef, bread crumbs, onion, milk, pepper, and salt. Shape this mixture into 20 meatballs. In a skillet, heat oil and brown the meatballs on all sides, then drain and transfer them to the Ninja Foodi PossibleCooker. 3. Add the cooked barley, celery, and peppers to the Ninja Foodi PossibleCooker. 4. In a separate bowl, combine the soup and water, then pour this mixture into the Ninja Foodi PossibleCooker. Gently mix all the ingredients together. 5. Dust the top with paprika for added flavor. 6. Cover the Ninja Foodi PossibleCooker and cook on low for 6 to 8 hours, or on high for 4 hours, until everything is heated through and flavors meld.

Cheesy Beef and Biscuit Bake

Prep time: 20 minutes | Cook time: 1 to 1½ hours | Serves 8

- 1½ pounds (680 g) extra-lean ground beef
- ½ cup chopped celery
- ½ cup chopped onions
- 2 tablespoons flour
- 1 teaspoon salt
- ¼ teaspoon black pepper
- ½ teaspoon dried oregano
- 2 (8-ounce / 227-g) cans tomato sauce
- 1 (10-ounce / 283-g) package frozen peas, thawed
- 2 (7½-ounce / 213-g) cans refrigerated buttermilk biscuits
- 2 cups fat-free shredded Cheddar cheese

1. Brown ground beef, celery, and onions in nonstick skillet. 2. Stir in flour, salt, pepper, and oregano. 3. Add tomato sauce and peas. 4. Pour into Ninja Foodi PossibleCooker. (A large oval cooker allows the biscuits to be arranged over top. You can also divide the mixture between two round Ninja Foodi PossibleCookers and accommodate the biscuits in that way.) 5. Arrange biscuits over top and sprinkle with cheese. 6. Cook uncovered on high for 1 to 1½ hours.

Sausage and Apples

Prep time: 10 minutes | Cook time: 1 to 3 hours | Serves 4

- 1 pound (454 g) smoked sausage
- 2 large apples, cored and
- sliced
- ¼ cup brown sugar
- ½ cup apple juice

1. Cut the meat into 2-inch pieces. 2. In the Ninja Foodi PossibleCooker, combine all the ingredients, mixing them thoroughly. 3. Cover and cook on low for 1 to 3 hours, or until everything is heated through and the apples reach your desired tenderness.

Apple-Raisin Ham

Prep time: 15 minutes | Cook time: 4 to 5 hours | Serves 6

- 1½ pounds (680 g) fully cooked ham
- 1 (21-ounce / 595-g) can apple pie filling
- ⅓ cup golden raisins
- ⅓ cup orange juice
- ¼ teaspoon ground cinnamon
- 2 tablespoons water

1. Slice the ham into six equal pieces. 2. In a mixing bowl, combine the pie filling, raisins, orange juice, cinnamon, and water. 3. Place one slice of ham in the Ninja Foodi PossibleCooker and top it with one-sixth of the apple mixture. 4. Continue layering the ham and apple mixture until all the ham and filling are used. 5. Cover the Ninja Foodi PossibleCooker and cook on low for 4 to 5 hours until heated through.

Ham-Broccoli Casserole

Prep time: 20 minutes | Cook time: 4 to 5 hours | Serves 4

- 1 (16-ounce / 454-g) package frozen broccoli cuts, thawed and drained
- 2 to 3 cups cubed, cooked ham
- 1 (10¾-ounce / 305-g) can cream of mushroom soup
- 4 ounces (113 g) of your favorite mild cheese, cubed
- 1 cup milk
- 1 cup instant rice, uncooked
- 1 rib celery, chopped
- 1 small onion, chopped

1. Place the broccoli and ham in the Ninja Foodi PossibleCooker, mixing them together. 2. In a separate bowl, combine the soup, cheese, milk, rice, celery, and onion, then stir this mixture into the broccoli and ham. 3. Cover the Ninja Foodi PossibleCooker and cook on low for 4 to 5 hours, until everything is heated through and the flavors meld.

Hearty Shiitake Beef Stew

Prep time: 10 minutes | Cook time: 8 to 9 hours | Serves 4 to 6

- 12 new potatoes, cut into quarters
- ½ cup chopped onions
- 1 (8-ounce / 227-g) package baby carrots
- 1 (3.4-ounce / 96-g) package fresh shiitake mushrooms, sliced, or 2 cups regular white mushrooms, sliced
- 1 (16-ounce / 454-g) can whole tomatoes
- 1 (14½-ounce / 411-g) can
- beef broth
- ½ cup flour
- 1 tablespoon Worcestershire sauce
- 1 teaspoon salt.
- 1 teaspoon sugar
- 1 teaspoon dried marjoram leaves
- ¼ teaspoon pepper
- 1 pound (454 g) beef stewing meat, cubed

1. Combine all ingredients except beef in Ninja Foodi PossibleCooker. Add beef. 2. Cover. Cook on low 8 to 9 hours. Stir well before serving.

Chinese Pot Roast

Prep time: 15 minutes | Cook time: 8¼ to 10¼ hours | Serves 6

- 1 (3-pound / 1.4-kg) boneless beef pot roast
- 2 tablespoons flour
- 1 tablespoon oil
- 2 large onions, chopped
- Salt to taste
- Pepper to taste
- ½ cup soy sauce
- 1 cup water
- ½ teaspoon ground ginger

1. Dredge the roast in flour, then brown it on both sides in oil in a saucepan. Transfer the browned roast to the Ninja Foodi PossibleCooker. 2. Layer the onions on top and season with salt and pepper. 3. In a bowl, mix together the soy sauce, water, and ginger, then pour this mixture over the meat. 4. Cover the Ninja Foodi PossibleCooker and cook on high for 10 minutes. Then, reduce the heat to low and cook for 8 to 10 hours until the meat is tender. 5. Slice the roast and serve.

Pork Chops and Stuffing with Curry

Prep time: 10 minutes | Cook time: 6 to 7 hours | Serves 3 to 4

- 1 box stuffing mix
- 1 cup water
- 1 (10¾-ounce / 305-g) can cream of mushroom soup
- 1 teaspoon, or more, curry powder, according to your taste preference
- 3 to 4 pork chops

1. Mix the stuffing with water and layer half of it on the bottom of the Ninja Foodi PossibleCooker. 2. In a separate bowl, combine the soup with curry powder and pour half of this mixture over the stuffing. Arrange the pork chops on top. 3. Spread the remaining stuffing over the pork chops and finish by pouring the rest of the soup mixture on top. 4. Cover and cook on low for 6 to 7 hours, until the pork is tender and fully cooked. 5. Serve warm and enjoy.

Smoky Chipotle Pulled Pork

Prep time: 15 minutes | Cook time: 6 hours | Serves 8

- 1 onion, finely chopped
- 2 teaspoon dried oregano
- 2 dried bay leaves
- 1 chipotle chile in adobo sauce, minced, plus 1 tablespoon sauce
- 1 (28-ounce / 794-g) can crushed tomatoes
- 1 (14½-ounce / 411-g) can whole tomatoes in puree
- 2 teaspoons coarse salt
- ½ teaspoon freshly ground pepper
- 2¾ pounds (1.3 kg) boneless pork shoulder, trimmed and halved crosswise

1. Preheat a 5- to 6-quart Ninja Foodi PossibleCooker. 2. Combine onion, oregano, bay leaves, chipotle and sauce, crushed and whole tomatoes (with puree), salt, and pepper in the Ninja Foodi PossibleCooker. Add pork and turn to coat completely. Cover and cook on high until meat is pull-apart tender, about 6 hours (or on low for 12 hours). 3. Transfer pork to a bowl and shred with two forks. Return pork to Ninja Foodi PossibleCooker and toss with sauce. Discard bay leaves.

Savory Turkey-Style Casserole

Prep time: 15 minutes | Cook time: 3 to 8 hours | Serves 6

- 2 pounds (907 g) hamburger, browned
- 1 teaspoon salt
- ½ teaspoon pepper
- 2 (10¾-ounce / 305-g) cans cream of chicken soup
- 1 (10¾-ounce / 305-g) can cream of celery soup
- 4 scant cups milk
- 1 large package bread stuffing or large loaf of bread, torn in pieces

1. Combine all ingredients in large buttered Ninja Foodi PossibleCooker. 2. Cover. Cook on high 3 hours, or on low 6 to 8 hours.

Chapter

4

Fish and Seafood

Chapter 4 Fish and Seafood

Cajun Shrimp & Sausage

Prep time: 15 minutes | Cook time: 3½ to 7 hours | Serves 6

- ¾ pound (340 g) andouille sausage, cut into ½-inch rounds (you may substitute Kiel-basa if you cannot find andouille sausage)
- 1 red onion, sliced into wedges
- 2 garlic cloves, minced
- 2 celery stalks, coarsely chopped
- 1 red or green bell pepper, coarsely chopped
- 2 tablespoons all-purpose flour
- 1 (28-ounce / 794-g) can diced tomatoes, with their juice
- ¼ teaspoon cayenne pepper
- Coarse sea salt
- ½ pound (227 g) large shrimp, peeled and deveined
- 2 cups fresh okra, sliced (you may substitute frozen and thawed, if necessary)

1. Put the sausage, onion, garlic, celery, and bell pepper into the Ninja Foodi PossibleCooker. Sprinkle with the flour and toss to coat. 2. Add the tomatoes and ½ cup water. Sprinkle with the cayenne pepper and season with salt. 3. Cover and cook on high for 3½ hours or on low for 7 hours, until the vegetables are tender. 4. Add the shrimp and okra. Cover and cook until the shrimp are opaque throughout, on high for 30 minutes or on low for 1 hour. Serve hot.

Garlic Tilapia

Prep time: 5 minutes | Cook time: 2 hours | Serves 4

- 2 tablespoons butter, at room temperature
- 2 cloves garlic, minced
- 2 teaspoons minced fresh
- flat-leaf parsley
- 4 tilapia fillets
- Sea salt
- Black pepper

1. In a small bowl, blend together the butter, garlic, and parsley until well combined. 2. Lay out a large sheet of aluminum foil on the counter and place the fish fillets in the center. 3. Season the fillets generously with salt and pepper. 4. Divide the butter mixture evenly among the fillets, placing it on top of each. 5. Fold the foil around the fish, sealing all sides and crimping the edges to create a packet. Place the packet in the Ninja Foodi PossibleCooker, cover, and cook on high for 2 hours. Serve while hot.

Bouillabaisse

Prep time: 25 minutes | Cook time: 7 to 9 hours | Serves 6 to 8

- ¼ cup extra-virgin olive oil
- 3 leeks, cleaned and coarsely chopped, using the white and tender green parts
- 4 cloves garlic, sliced
- 1 bulb fennel, ends trimmed, coarsely chopped
- Grated zest of 1 orange
- 1 teaspoon dried thyme
- 1 teaspoon saffron threads, crushed
- Pinch of cayenne pepper
- 1 (28- to 32-ounce / 794- to
- 907-g) can crushed tomatoes, with their juice
- ½ cup white wine or dry vermouth
- 3 cups clam juice
- 1 cup chicken broth
- ½ pound (227 g) littleneck clams
- ½ pound (227 g) mussels
- 3 pounds (1.4 kg) thick-fleshed fish, cut into 1-inch chunks
- ½ cup finely chopped fresh Italian parsley

1. In a large skillet, heat oil over medium-high heat. Add the leeks, garlic, fennel, zest, thyme, saffron, and cayenne, and sauté until the vegetables soften, about 2 minutes. Incorporate the tomatoes and wine, cooking for 10 minutes to enhance the flavors. Transfer this mixture to the insert of a 5- to 7-quart Ninja Foodi PossibleCooker. 2. Pour in the clam juice and broth, stirring to combine everything well. Cover and cook on low for 6 to 8 hours. When ready, remove the lid and add the clams and mussels to the sauce. 3. Place the fish on top of the shellfish, then ladle the sauce over the fish. Cover and cook on high for 45 minutes, until the fish is opaque and the clams and mussels have opened. 4. Discard any shellfish that remain closed. Garnish with parsley and serve immediately.

Shrimp & Artichoke Barley Risotto

Prep time: 15 minutes | Cook time: 3 hours | Serves 4

- 3 cups seafood stock (or chicken stock)
- 1 teaspoon olive oil
- 1 yellow onion, chopped
- 3 cloves garlic, minced
- 1 (9-ounce / 255-g) package frozen artichoke hearts, thawed and quartered
- 1 cup uncooked pearl barley
- Black pepper
- 1 pound (454 g) shrimp, peeled and deveined
- 2 ounces (57 g) Parmesan or Pecorino Romano cheese, grated
- 2 teaspoons lemon zest
- 4 ounces (113 g) fresh baby spinach

1. Bring the stock to a boil in a medium saucepan. Remove from the heat and set aside. 2. In a nonstick medium skillet over medium-high heat, heat the olive oil. Add the onion and sauté until tender, about 5 minutes. Add the garlic and sauté for 1 more minute. 3. Transfer the onion and garlic to the Ninja Foodi PossibleCooker and add the artichoke hearts and barley. Season with some pepper. Stir in the seafood stock. 4. Cover and cook on high for 3 hours, or until the barley is tender and the liquid is just about all absorbed. 5. About 15 minutes before the cooking time is completed, stir in the shrimp and grated cheese. Cover and continue to cook on high for another 10 minutes, or until the shrimp are opaque. 6. Add the lemon zest and fold in the baby spinach, stirring until it's wilted, about 1 minute. 7. Divide the risotto among the serving bowls and serve hot.

Catalan-Style Seafood Stew

Prep time: 20 minutes | Cook time: 7 hours | Serves 6 to 8

- ½ cup extra-virgin olive oil
- 2 medium onions, finely chopped
- 2 medium red bell peppers, seeded and finely chopped
- 6 cloves garlic, minced
- 1 teaspoon saffron threads, crushed
- 1 teaspoon hot paprika
- 1 cup finely chopped Spanish chorizo or soppressata salami
- 1 (28- to 32-ounce / 794- to 907-g) can crushed tomatoes
- 2 cups clam juice
- 1 cup chicken broth
- 2 pounds (907 g) firm-fleshed fish, such as halibut, monkfish, cod, or sea bass fillets, cut into 1-inch chunks
- 1½ pounds (680 g) littleneck clams
- ½ cup finely chopped fresh Italian parsley

1. In a large skillet, heat the oil over medium-high heat. Add the onions, bell peppers, garlic, saffron, paprika, and chorizo, and sauté until the vegetables are softened, about 5 to 7 minutes. Stir in the tomatoes, then transfer the mixture to the insert of a 5- to 7-quart Ninja Foodi PossibleCooker. Add the clam juice and broth, stirring to combine. 2. Cover the Ninja Foodi PossibleCooker and cook on low for 6 hours. Once done, add the fish and clams to the insert, spooning some sauce over the fish and pushing the clams beneath the sauce. 3. Cover again and cook for an additional 45 to 50 minutes, until the clams have opened and the fish is fully cooked and opaque. Discard any clams that remain closed. 4. Garnish the stew with parsley and serve immediately.

Pacifica Sweet-Hot Salmon

Prep time: 10 minutes | Cook time: 1½ hours | Serves 6

- 3 pounds (1.4 kg) salmon fillets
- ½ cup Colman's English mustard
- ¼ cup honey
- 2 tablespoons finely chopped fresh dill

1. Arrange the salmon in the insert of a 5- to 7-quart Ninja Foodi PossibleCooker. In a small bowl, mix together the mustard, honey, and dill until well combined. 2. Pour the mustard mixture over the salmon, spreading it evenly across the surface. 3. Cover and cook on high for 1½ hours, or until the salmon is fully cooked. 4. Serve the salmon directly from the Ninja Foodi PossibleCooker, drizzled with some of the sauce.

Honey-Lime Glazed Salmon

Prep time: 10 minutes | Cook time: 1 hour | Serves 6

- 6 (6-ounce / 170-g) salmon fillets
- ½ cup honey
- 2 tablespoons lime juice
- 3 tablespoons Worcestershire
- sauce
- 1 tablespoon water
- 2 cloves garlic, minced
- 1 teaspoon ground ginger
- ½ teaspoon black pepper

1. Place the salmon fillets in the Ninja Foodi PossibleCooker. 2. In medium bowl, whisk the honey, lime juice, Worcestershire sauce, water, garlic, ginger, and pepper. Pour sauce over salmon. 3. Cover and cook on high for 1 hour.

Poached Salmon Cakes in White Wine Butter Sauce

Prep time: 15 minutes | Cook time: 5 hours | Serves 6

White Wine Butter Sauce:

- ½ cup (1 stick) unsalted butter
- 1 teaspoon Old Bay seasoning

- 2 cloves garlic, sliced
- 2 ½ cups white wine or vermouth

Salmon Cakes:

- 4 cups cooked salmon, flaked
- 1 (6-ounce / 170-g) jar marinated artichoke hearts, drained and coarsely chopped
- 1 cup fresh bread crumbs

- ½ cup freshly grated Parmigiano-Reggiano cheese
- 1 large egg, beaten
- ½ teaspoon freshly ground black pepper

1. In the insert of a 5- to 7-quart Ninja Foodi PossibleCooker, combine all the sauce ingredients and stir well. Cover and cook on low for 4 hours. 2. In a large mixing bowl, combine all the ingredients for the salmon cakes and mix until well blended. Shape the mixture into 2-inch cakes. Place the cakes into the simmering sauce, spooning some sauce over the top. 3. Cover and cook for an additional hour, or until the cakes are tender. Carefully transfer the cakes to a serving platter. 4. Strain the sauce through a fine-mesh sieve into a saucepan. Bring the strained sauce to a boil and reduce it by half. 5. Serve the sauce drizzled over the cakes or on the side as a dip.

Spicy BBQ Scallops & Shrimp

Prep time: 20 minutes | Cook time: 1 hour | Serves 2

- ½ teaspoon paprika
- ½ teaspoon garlic powder
- ¼ teaspoon onion powder
- ¼ teaspoon cayenne pepper
- ¼ teaspoon dried oregano
- ¼ teaspoon dried thyme
- ½ teaspoon sea salt
- ½ teaspoon black pepper
- 2 cloves garlic, minced

- ½ cup olive oil
- ¼ cup Worcestershire sauce
- 1 tablespoon hot pepper sauce (like Tabasco)
- Juice of 1 lemon
- 1 pound (454 g) scallops
- 1 pound (454 g) large shrimp, unpeeled
- 1 green onion, finely chopped

1. Combine the paprika, garlic powder, onion powder, cayenne pepper, oregano, thyme, ½ teaspoon salt, and ¼ teaspoon black pepper. 2. Combine the paprika blend, garlic, olive oil, Worcestershire sauce, hot pepper sauce, and lemon juice in the Ninja Foodi PossibleCooker. Season with salt and pepper. 3. Cover and cook on high for 30 minutes or until hot. 4. Rinse the scallops and shrimp, and drain. 5. Spoon one-half of the sauce from the Ninja Foodi PossibleCooker into a glass measuring cup. 6. Place the scallops and shrimp in the Ninja Foodi PossibleCooker with the remaining sauce. Drizzle with the sauce in the measuring cup, and stir to coat. 7. Cover and cook on high for 30 minutes, until the scallops and shrimp are opaque. 8. Turn the heat to warm for serving. Sprinkle with the chopped green onion to serve.

Mahi-Mahi with Tropical Salsa & Lentils

Prep time: 30 minutes | Cook time: 6 hours | Serves 6

- 1¼ cups vegetable or chicken stock
- 1 cup orange juice
- ¾ cup orange lentils
- ½ cup finely diced carrot
- ¼ cup finely diced red onion
- ¼ cup finely diced celery

- 1 tablespoon honey
- 6 (4- to-5-ounce / 113- to 142-g) mahi-mahi fillets
- Sea salt
- Black pepper
- 1 teaspoon lemon juice

Salsa:

- ¾ cup finely diced pineapple
- ¾ cup finely diced mango
- ½ cup finely diced strawberries
- ¼ cup finely diced red onion

- 2 tablespoons chopped fresh mint (or 2 teaspoons dried)
- 2 tablespoons orange juice
- 1 tablespoon lime juice
- ¼ teaspoon salt

1. Combine the stock, orange juice, lentils, carrot, onion, celery, and honey in the Ninja Foodi PossibleCooker. 2. Cover and cook on low for 5 to 5½ hours, or until the lentils are tender. 3. Place 1 sheet of parchment paper over the lentils in the Ninja Foodi PossibleCooker. Season mahi-mahi lightly with salt and black pepper and place it on the parchment (skin-side down, if you have not removed the skin). Replace the lid and continue to cook on low for 25 minutes or until the mahi-mahi is opaque in the center. Remove the fish by lifting out the parchment paper and putting it on a plate. 4. Stir the lemon juice into the lentils and season with salt and pepper. Make the Salsa: 5. While the fish is cooking, combine the pineapple, mango, strawberries, red onion, mint, orange juice, lime juice, and salt into a big jar. Combine and chill to give the flavors a chance to blend. 6. To serve, place about ½ cup of hot lentils on a plate and top with a mahimahi fillet and ⅓ cup of salsa.

Citrus Swordfish

Prep time: 15 minutes | Cook time: 1½ hours | Serves 2

- Nonstick cooking oil spray
- 1½ pounds (680 g) swordfish fillets
- Sea salt
- Black pepper
- 1 yellow onion, chopped
- 5 tablespoons chopped fresh flat-leaf parsley
- 1 tablespoon olive oil
- 2 teaspoons lemon zest
- 2 teaspoons orange zest
- Orange and lemon slices, for garnish
- Fresh parsley sprigs, for garnish

1. Spray the inside of the Ninja Foodi PossibleCooker crock with nonstick cooking oil. 2. Season the fish fillets with salt and pepper and place them in the Ninja Foodi PossibleCooker. 3. Top the fish with the onion, parsley, olive oil, lemon zest, and orange zest, distributing them evenly. 4. Cover the Ninja Foodi PossibleCooker and cook on low for 1½ hours. 5. Serve the fish hot, garnished with slices of orange and lemon, along with fresh parsley sprigs.

Potato-Crusted Sea Bass Delight

Prep time: 15 minutes | Cook time: 1½ hours | Serves 6

- 1 cup (2 sticks) unsalted butter, melted and cooled
- ½ cup fresh lemon juice
- Grated zest of 1 lemon
- 2 cloves garlic, minced
- 8 tablespoons olive oil
- 2 tablespoons Old Bay seasoning
- 2 to 3 pounds (907 g to 1.4 kg) sea bass fillets, cut to fit the slow-cooker insert
- 6 medium Yukon gold potatoes, cut into ¼-inch-thick slices

1. Stir the butter, lemon juice, zest, garlic, and 2 tablespoons of the olive oil together in a small bowl. Combine the remaining 6 tablespoons oil and the seasoning in a large mixing bowl. 2. Paint the sea bass with some of the butter sauce and set aside. Toss the potatoes in the seasoned oil. Pour half the butter sauce in the insert of a 5- to 7-quart Ninja Foodi PossibleCooker. 3. Place half the potatoes in the bottom of the Ninja Foodi PossibleCooker. Place the sea bass on top of the potatoes and pour half the remaining butter sauce over the sea bass. Place the remaining potatoes on top of the sea bass and drizzle with the remaining butter sauce. 4. Cover and cook on high for 1½ hours, until the potatoes begin to turn golden and the sea bass is cooked through and opaque in the middle. Remove the cover and cook for an additional 15 to 20 minutes. 5. Serve immediately.

Bayou Gulf Shrimp Gumbo

Prep time: 35 minutes | Cook time: 5 hours | Serves 6

- ½ pound (227 g) bacon strips, chopped
- 3 celery ribs, chopped
- 1 medium onion, chopped
- 1 medium green pepper, chopped
- 2 garlic cloves, minced
- 2 (8-ounce / 227-g) bottles clam juice
- 1 (14½-ounce / 411-g) can diced tomatoes, undrained
- 2 tablespoons Worcestershire sauce
- 1 teaspoon kosher salt
- 1 teaspoon dried marjoram
- 2 pounds (907 g) uncooked large shrimp, peeled and deveined
- 2½ cups frozen sliced okra, thawed
- Hot cooked rice

1. In a large skillet, cook the bacon over medium heat until crispy. Remove with a slotted spoon and place on paper towels to drain, reserving 2 tablespoons of the drippings. Sauté the celery, onion, green pepper, and garlic in the reserved drippings until tender. 2. Transfer the mixture to a 4-quart Ninja Foodi PossibleCooker. Add the bacon, clam juice, tomatoes, Worcestershire sauce, salt, and marjoram, stirring to combine. Cover and cook on low for 4 hours. 3. Add the shrimp and okra to the Ninja Foodi PossibleCooker, cover, and cook for an additional hour, or until the shrimp are pink and the okra is heated through. Serve over rice.

Acadiana BBQ Shrimp

Prep time: 15 minutes | Cook time: 4 hours | Serves 6 to 8

- 1 cup (2 sticks) unsalted butter
- ¼ cup olive oil
- 8 cloves garlic, sliced
- 2 teaspoons dried oregano
- 1 teaspoon dried thyme
- ½ teaspoon freshly ground black pepper
- Pinch of cayenne pepper
- 2 teaspoons sweet paprika
- ¼ cup Worcestershire sauce
- ¼ cup lemon juice
- 3 pounds (1.4 kg) large shrimp, peeled and deveined
- ½ cup finely chopped fresh Italian parsley

1. Put the butter, oil, garlic, oregano, thyme, pepper, cayenne, paprika, Worcestershire, and lemon juice in the insert of a 5- to 7-quart Ninja Foodi PossibleCooker. Cover and cook on low for 4 hours. 2. Turn the cooker up to high and add the shrimp, tossing them in the butter sauce. Cover and cook for an additional 10 to 5 minutes, until the shrimp are pink. 3. Transfer the shrimp from the Ninja Foodi PossibleCooker to a large serving bowl and pour the sauce over the shrimp. Sprinkle with the parsley and serve.

Simple Poached Turbot

Prep time: 10 minutes | Cook time: 40 to 50 minutes | Serves 4

- 1 cup vegetable or chicken stock
- ½ cup dry white wine
- 1 yellow onion, sliced
- 1 lemon, sliced
- 4 sprigs fresh dill
- ½ teaspoon sea salt
- 4 (6-ounce / 170-g) turbot fillets

1. In the Ninja Foodi PossibleCooker, combine the stock and wine. Cover and heat on high for 20 to 30 minutes. 2. Add the onion, lemon, dill, salt, and turbot to the mixture. Cover and cook on high for about 20 minutes, or until the turbot is opaque and cooked to your liking. Serve hot.

Seafood Laksa

Prep time: 30 minutes | Cook time: 2½ hours | Serves 6 to 8

- 2 tablespoons virgin coconut oil or extra-virgin olive oil
- 1 small onion, chopped
- 4 Thai bird chiles
- 1 (2-inch) piece fresh ginger, peeled and grated
- 1 (1-inch) piece fresh turmeric, peeled and grated
- 1 lemongrass stalk, tough outer leaves discarded, inner bulb chopped
- ¼ cup fresh cilantro
- 1 tablespoon tamarind paste
- ½ teaspoon ground cumin
- ½ teaspoon paprika
- 2 teaspoon coarse salt
- 2 cups unsweetened coconut milk
- 2 cups boiling water
- 4 kaffir lime leaves
- 2 teaspoon fish sauce
- 1 pound (454 g) medium shrimp, peeled and deveined (shells rinsed and reserved)
- 2 pounds (907 g) small mussels, scrubbed
- ¾ pound (340 g) firm fish fillet, such as halibut or cod, cut into 1-inch pieces
- 8 ounces (227 g) rice noodles
- Lime wedges, cubed firm tofu, sliced scallions, sliced Thai bird chiles, cilantro, and chili oil, for serving

1. Preheat a 7-quart Ninja Foodi PossibleCooker. 2. Heat oil in a saucepan over medium. Add onion and cook until translucent, about 5 minutes. Add chiles, ginger, turmeric, lemongrass, cilantro, tamarind paste, cumin, paprika, and salt. Cook until fragrant, about 2 more minutes. Remove from heat and let cool. Transfer spice mixture to a food processor and puree to a thick paste. 3. Combine laksa paste, coconut milk, the boiling water, lime leaves, fish sauce, and shrimp shells in the Ninja Foodi PossibleCooker. Cover and cook on low for 2 hours (we prefer this recipe on low). 4. Strain liquid through a medium sieve into a bowl, pressing down on solids; return broth to Ninja Foodi PossibleCooker (discard solids). Add shrimp and mussels, and cook on low 20 minutes. Add fish and cook until shrimp is completely cooked through, fish is firm, and mussels open, about 10 minutes. 5. Meanwhile, prepare noodles according to package instructions. 6. To serve, divide noodles among bowls. Add broth and seafood, and top with tofu, scallions, chiles, and cilantro. Serve with lime wedges and chili oil.

Moroccan-Spiced Sea Bass

Prep time: 20 minutes | Cook time: 3 to 4 hours | Serves 8

- 2 tablespoons extra-virgin olive oil
- 1 large yellow onion, finely chopped
- 1 medium red bell pepper, cut into ½-inch strips
- 1 medium yellow bell pepper, cut into ½-inch strips
- 4 garlic cloves, minced
- 1 teaspoon saffron threads, crushed in the palm of your hand
- 1½ teaspoons sweet paprika
- ¼ teaspoon hot paprika or ¼ teaspoon smoked paprika (or pimentón)
- ½ teaspoon ground ginger
- 1 (15-ounce / 425-g) can diced tomatoes, with the juice
- ¼ cup fresh orange juice
- 2 pounds (907 g) fresh sea bass fillets
- ¼ cup finely chopped fresh flat-leaf parsley
- ¼ cup finely chopped fresh cilantro
- Sea salt
- Black pepper
- 1 navel orange, thinly sliced, for garnish

1. In a large skillet, heat the olive oil over medium-high heat. Add the onion, red and yellow bell peppers, garlic, saffron, sweet paprika, hot or smoked paprika, and ginger and cook, stirring often, for 3 minutes, or until the onion begins to soften. 2. Add the tomatoes and stir for another 2 minutes, to blend the flavors. 3. Transfer the mixture to the Ninja Foodi PossibleCooker and stir in the orange juice. 4. Place the sea bass fillets on top of the tomato mixture, and spoon some of the mixture over the fish. Cover and cook on high for 2 hours, or on low for 3 to 4 hours. At the end of the cooking time, the sea bass should be opaque in the center. 5. Carefully lift the fish out of the Ninja Foodi PossibleCooker with a spatula and transfer to a serving platter. Cover loosely with aluminum foil. 6. Skim off any excess fat from the sauce, stir in the parsley and cilantro, and season with salt and pepper. 7. Spoon some of the sauce over the fish, and garnish with the orange slices. Serve hot, passing the remaining sauce on the side.

Beantown Buttered Scallops

Prep time: 10 minutes | Cook time: 4½ hours | Serves 6

- 1 cup (2 sticks) unsalted butter
- 2 tablespoons olive oil
- 2 cloves garlic, minced
- 2 teaspoons sweet paprika
- ¼ cup dry sherry
- 2 pounds (907 g) dry-pack sea scallops
- ½ cup finely chopped fresh Italian parsley

1. Put the butter, oil, garlic, paprika, and sherry in the insert of a 5- to 7-quart slower cooker. 2. Cover and cook on low for 4 hours. Turn the cooker to high and add the scallops, tossing them in the butter sauce. Cover and cook on high for 30 to 40 minutes, until the scallops are opaque. 3. Transfer the scallops and sauce from the Ninja Foodi PossibleCooker to a serving platter. Sprinkle with the parsley and serve.

Halibut with Eggplant and Ginger Relish

Prep time: 25 minutes | Cook time: 4 hours | Serves 4

- 4 medium Japanese eggplants (or 2 large eggplants), cut into ½-inch cubes
- ¼ cup coarse salt
- ¼ cup extra-virgin olive oil
- 2 onions, diced
- 3 garlic cloves, minced
- 1 (1-inch) piece fresh ginger, peeled and finely grated
- 2 kaffir lime leaves
- 2 teaspoon brown sugar
- 1 tablespoon rice vinegar
- ¼ cup fresh lime juice
- 1 cup packed fresh cilantro, finely chopped
- 1 pound (454 g) halibut, cut into 1-inch pieces
- ½ cup unsweetened flaked coconut, toasted, for garnish

1. Place the eggplant in a colander, sprinkle with salt, and let it sit over a bowl for about an hour. Rinse thoroughly and pat dry. 2. Preheat a 5- to 6-quart Ninja Foodi PossibleCooker. 3. In a large skillet, heat 2 tablespoons of oil over medium heat. Add the onions and sauté until deeply golden, about 15 minutes. Stir in the garlic and ginger, cooking for an additional 2 minutes. Then, add the eggplant and cook until heated through. Transfer the vegetable mixture to the Ninja Foodi PossibleCooker. 4. In the Ninja Foodi PossibleCooker, add the remaining 2 tablespoons of oil, lime leaves, brown sugar, vinegar, and lime juice. Cover and cook on low for about 4 hours, or on high for 2 hours, until the vegetables are very soft but not mushy. 5. Stir in cilantro, then place the fish on top of the eggplant mixture. Cover and cook on low until the fish is cooked through, about 20 minutes, or on high for 10 minutes. Serve the relish topped with halibut and garnished with toasted coconut.

Poached Salmon Provenc

Prep time: 15 minutes | Cook time: 1½ to 2 hours | Serves 6

- 3 pounds (1.4 kg) salmon fillets
- ½ cup dry white wine or vermouth
- 4 cloves garlic, peeled
- 1½ teaspoons finely chopped fresh rosemary
- 2 teaspoons finely chopped fresh thyme leaves
- 2 teaspoons finely chopped fresh tarragon
- ½ cup olive oil
- 1 (28- to 32-ounce / 794- to 907-g) can plum tomatoes, drained
- ½ cup heavy cream
- Salt and freshly ground black pepper

1. Place the salmon in the insert of a 5- to 7-quart Ninja Foodi PossibleCooker and pour the white wine over it. 2. In a food processor, combine the garlic, rosemary, thyme, tarragon, oil, and tomatoes, then blend until smooth. Spoon this mixture over the salmon in the Ninja Foodi PossibleCooker. 3. Cover and cook on high for 1½ to 2 hours, or until the salmon is fully cooked. 4. Carefully transfer the salmon to a serving platter and remove the skin. Pour the sauce into a saucepan and bring it to a boil, reducing it by about ¼ cup. Stir in the heavy cream and season with salt and pepper. 5. Serve the salmon topped with the sauce.

Lemon, Garlic, and Butter Halibut

Prep time: 15 minutes | Cook time: 5 hours | Serves 6

- 1 cup (2 sticks) unsalted butter
- ½ cup olive oil
- 6 cloves garlic, sliced
- 1 teaspoon sweet paprika
- ½ cup lemon juice
- Grated zest of 1 lemon
- ¼ cup finely chopped fresh chives
- 2 to 3 pounds (907 g to 1.4 kg) halibut fillets
- ½ cup finely chopped fresh Italian parsley

1. In the insert of a 5- to 7-quart Ninja Foodi PossibleCooker, mix together the butter, oil, garlic, paprika, lemon juice, zest, and chives. Stir to combine, then cover and cook on low for 4 hours. 2. Place the halibut in the pot, spooning some sauce over the top. Cover and cook for an additional 40 minutes, or until the halibut is opaque and fully cooked. 3. Garnish the fish with parsley and serve immediately.

Scallop & Crab Cioppino

Prep time: 15 minutes | Cook time: 7 hours | Serves 4

- Cooking oil spray
- 1 medium yellow onion, finely chopped
- 4 cloves garlic, minced
- 1 (15-ounce / 425-g) can diced tomatoes, with the juice
- 1 (10-ounce / 283-g) can diced tomatoes with green chiles
- 2 cups seafood stock
- 1 cup red wine
- 3 tablespoons chopped fresh basil
- 2 bay leaves
- 1 pound (454 g) cooked crab meat, shredded
- 1½ pounds (680 g) scallops
- Sea salt
- Black pepper
- ¼ cup fresh flat-leaf parsley, for garnish

1. Coat a large sauté pan with cooking oil spray and heat over medium-high heat. Add the onion and sauté for about 5 minutes, until softened. 2. Add the garlic and sauté until golden and fragrant, about 2 minutes. 3. Transfer the onion and garlic to the Ninja Foodi PossibleCooker, and add the tomatoes, tomatoes with green chiles, stock, wine, basil, and bay leaves. Cover and cook on low for 6 hours. 4. About 30 minutes before the cooking time is completed, add the crab meat and scallops. Cover and cook on high for 30 minutes. The seafood will turn opaque. Season to taste with salt and pepper. Serve hot, garnished with parsley.

Spicy Tomato Basil Mussels

Prep time: 15 minutes | Cook time: 7 hours | Serves 4

- 3 tablespoons olive oil
- 4 cloves garlic, minced
- 3 shallot cloves, minced
- 8 ounces (227 g) mushrooms, diced
- 1 (28-ounce / 794-g) can diced tomatoes, with the juice
- ¾ cup white wine
- 2 tablespoons dried oregano
- ½ tablespoon dried basil
- ½ teaspoon black pepper
- 1 teaspoon paprika
- ¼ teaspoon red pepper flakes
- 3 pounds (1.4 kg) mussels

1. In a large sauté pan, heat olive oil over medium-high heat. Add the garlic, shallots, and mushrooms, cooking for 2 to 3 minutes until the garlic is lightly browned and fragrant. Transfer everything from the pan into the Ninja Foodi PossibleCooker. 2. In the Ninja Foodi PossibleCooker, add the tomatoes and white wine, then sprinkle in the oregano, basil, black pepper, paprika, and red pepper flakes. 3. Cover and cook on low for 4 to 5 hours, or on high for 2 to 3 hours, until the mushrooms are fork-tender. 4. Clean and debeard the mussels, discarding any that are already open. 5. Once the mushroom mixture is ready, increase the heat on the Ninja Foodi PossibleCooker to high. Add the cleaned mussels, cover tightly, and cook for an additional 30 minutes. 6. To serve, ladle the mussels into bowls along with plenty of broth, discarding any mussels that haven't opened. Enjoy hot, ideally with crusty bread for dipping in the sauce.

Olive Oil Poached Tuna

Prep time: 5 minutes | Cook time: 3 to 4 hours | Serves 6

- 3 pounds (1.4 kg) tuna fillets
- Olive oil to cover the fish
- 1 teaspoon coarse sea salt

1. Place the tuna in the insert of a 5- to 7-quart Ninja Foodi PossibleCooker and pour the oil over the tuna. The oil should cover the tuna, and depending on the shape of your Ninja Foodi PossibleCooker, you may need to add a bit more oil. Add the salt to the slow-cooker insert. 2. Cover and cook on low for 3 to 4 hours, until the tuna is cooked through and is white. Remove the tuna from the oil and cool completely before using.

Miso-Poached Salmon

Prep time: 10 minutes | Cook time: 1½ hours | Serves 8

- 3 pounds (1.4 kg) salmon fillets
- 3 tablespoons white miso
- 3 tablespoons honey
- ¼ cup rice wine (mirin) or dry sherry
- 2 teaspoons freshly grated ginger

1. place the salmon in the insert of a 5- to 7-quart Ninja Foodi PossibleCooker. 2. Combine the miso, honey, rice wine, and ginger in a mixing bowl and stir. 3. Pour the sauce over the salmon in the Ninja Foodi PossibleCooker. Cover and cook on high for 1½ hours, until the salmon is cooked through and registers 165°F (74°C) on an instant-read thermometer inserted in the center of a thick fillet. 4. Carefully remove the salmon from the slow-cooker insert with a large spatula. Remove the skin from the underside of the salmon (if necessary) and arrange the salmon on a serving platter. 5. Strain the sauce through a fine-mesh sieve into a saucepan. Boil the sauce, reduce it to a syrupy consistency, and serve with the salmon.

Shrimp Marinara

Prep time: 15 minutes | Cook time: 6 to 7 hours | Serves 4

- 1 (15-ounce / 425-g) can diced tomatoes, with the juice
- 1 (6-ounce / 170-g) can tomato paste
- 1 clove garlic, minced
- 2 tablespoons minced fresh flat-leaf parsley
- ½ teaspoon dried basil
- 1 teaspoon dried oregano
- 1 teaspoon garlic powder
- 1½ teaspoons sea salt
- ¼ teaspoon black pepper
- 1 pound (454 g) cooked shrimp, peeled and deveined
- 2 cups hot cooked spaghetti or linguine, for serving
- ½ cup grated Parmesan cheese, for serving

1. Combine the tomatoes, tomato paste, and minced garlic in the Ninja Foodi PossibleCooker. Sprinkle with the parsley, basil, oregano, garlic powder, salt, and pepper. 2. Cover and cook on low for 6 to 7 hours. 3. Turn up the heat to high, stir in the cooked shrimp, and cover and cook on high for about 15 minutes longer. 4. Serve hot over the cooked pasta. Top with Parmesan cheese.

Low Country Slow-Cooker Seafood Boil

Prep time: 15 minutes | Cook time: 6 hours | Serves 8

- 8 medium red potatoes
- 2 large, sweet onions, such as Vidalia, quartered
- 2 pounds (907 g) smoked sausage, cut into 3-inch pieces
- 1 (3-ounce / 85-g) package seafood boil seasoning
- 1 (12-ounce / 340-g) bottle pale ale beer
- 10 cups water
- 4 ears of corn, halved
- 2 pounds (907 g) medium raw shrimp, shelled and deveined
- Cocktail sauce, for serving
- Hot sauce, for serving
- ½ cup melted butter, for serving
- 1 large lemon, cut into wedges, for garnish

1. In the Ninja Foodi PossibleCooker, put the potatoes, onions, smoked sausage, seafood boil seasoning, beer, and water. Stir to combine. Cover and cook for 6 hours, or until the potatoes are tender when pierced with a fork. 2. About 45 minutes before serving, add the corn. Cover and continue cooking for 25 minutes. Add the shrimp, cover, and continue cooking until the shrimp are pink and no longer translucent. 3. Drain the Ninja Foodi PossibleCooker, discard the cooking liquid, and serve the seafood with cocktail sauce, hot sauce, melted butter, and lemon wedges.

Smoked Salmon and Potato Casserole

Prep time: 10 minutes | Cook time: 8 hours | Serves 2

- 1 teaspoon butter, at room temperature, or extra-virgin olive oil
- 2 eggs
- 1 cup 2% milk
- 1 teaspoon dried dill
- ⅛ teaspoon sea salt
- Freshly ground black pepper
- 2 medium russet potatoes, peeled and sliced thin
- 4 ounces (113 g) smoked salmon

1. Grease the inside of the Ninja Foodi PossibleCooker with butter. 2. In a small bowl, whisk together the eggs, milk, dill, salt, and a few grinds of black pepper. 3. Layer one-third of the potatoes on the bottom of the Ninja Foodi PossibleCooker, followed by one-third of the salmon. Pour one-third of the egg mixture over the salmon. Repeat these layers with the remaining potatoes, salmon, and egg mixture. 4. Cover and cook on low for 8 hours or overnight.

Miso-Glazed Cod

Prep time: 15 minutes | Cook time: 5 hours | Serves 6

- ½ cup white miso paste
- ¼ cup rice wine (mirin)
- ¼ firmly packed light brown sugar
- 1 teaspoon rice vinegar
- 1 ½ cups water
- 2 pounds (907 g) black cod (if unavailable, use fresh cod, halibut, sea bass, or salmon)
- 6 green onions, finely chopped, using the white and tender green parts
- ¼ cup toasted sesame seeds for garnish

1. In the insert of a 5- to 7-quart Ninja Foodi PossibleCooker, mix together the miso, rice wine, sugar, rice vinegar, and water. 2. Cover and cook on low for 4 hours. Then, add the cod, spooning some sauce over the fish. Cover and cook for an additional 30 to 45 minutes. 3. Carefully remove the cod from the Ninja Foodi PossibleCooker and cover it with aluminum foil to keep warm. Pour the sauce into a saucepan, bring it to a boil, and reduce until syrupy, about 15 to 20 minutes. Stir in the green onions. 4. Serve each piece of cod in a pool of the sauce, sprinkling with sesame seeds. Offer any extra sauce on the side.

South-of-the-Border Halibut

Prep time: 10 minutes | Cook time: 3½ hours | Serves 6

- 3 cups prepared medium-hot salsa
- 2 tablespoons fresh lime juice
- 1 teaspoon ground cumin
- 2 to 3 pounds (907 g to 1.4 kg) halibut fillets
- 1½ cup finely shredded Monterey Jack cheese (or Pepper Jack for a spicy topping)

1. In the insert of a 5- to 7-quart Ninja Foodi PossibleCooker, mix together the salsa, lime juice, and cumin. Cover and cook on low for 2 hours. 2. Add the halibut to the cooker, spooning some sauce over the fish. Evenly sprinkle the cheese on top. Cover and cook for an additional 30 to 45 minutes. 3. Carefully remove the halibut from the Ninja Foodi PossibleCooker and serve it on a bed of the sauce.

Chapter

5

Poultry

Chapter 5 Poultry

Sweet Marmalade Chicken

Prep time: 15 minutes | Cook time: 5 to 6 hours | Serves 6 to 8

- 2 medium raw sweet potatoes, peeled and cut into ¼-inch thick slices
- 8 boneless, skinless chicken thighs
- 1 (8-ounce / 227-g) jar orange marmalade
- ¼ cup water
- ¼ to ½ teaspoon salt
- ½ teaspoon pepper

1. Place sweet potato slices in Ninja Foodi PossibleCooker. 2. Rinse and dry chicken pieces. Arrange on top of the potatoes. 3. Spoon marmalade over the chicken and potatoes. 4. Pour water over all. Season with salt and pepper. 5. Cover and cook on high 1 hour, and then turn to low and cook 4 to 5 hours, or until potatoes and chicken are both tender.

Moroccan Fruited Chicken Tagine

Prep time: 25 minutes | Cook time: 5 to 6 hours | Serves 6

- 8 chicken thighs, skin and bones removed
- 1½ teaspoons salt
- ⅛ teaspoon cayenne
- ¼ cup olive oil
- 1 medium onion, coarsely chopped
- 1 teaspoon ground turmeric
- 2 cloves garlic, minced
- ½ teaspoon ground cumin
- ½ teaspoon ground ginger
- 1 tablespoon brown sugar
- ½ cup dried apricots, cut into quarters
- ½ cup dried plums
- ½ cup orange juice
- Grated zest of one orange
- 1½ cups chicken broth
- ¼ cup water mixed with 2 tablespoons cornstarch
- 3 cups cooked couscous

1. Sprinkle the chicken with the salt and cayenne. Heat the oil in a large skillet over high heat. Add the chicken a few pieces at a time and brown on all sides. 2. Transfer the browned chicken to the insert of a 5- to 7-quart Ninja Foodi PossibleCooker. Add the onion, turmeric, garlic, cumin, ginger, and brown sugar to the skillet and sauté until the onion begin to soften, about 4 minutes.

3. Transfer the contents of the skillet to the slow-cooker insert. Add the apricots, plums, orange juice, orange zest, and broth to the cooker. Cover and cook on high for 4½ to 5½ hours, until the chicken is tender and the fruit is plump. 4. Stir in the cornstarch mixture and cook for an additional 30 to 45 minutes, until the sauce is thickened. 5. Serve the chicken, fruit, and sauce over a bed of the couscous.

Tender Turkey Breast

Prep time: 5 minutes | Cook time: 2 to 9 hours | Serves 10

- 1 (6-pound / 2.7-kg) boneless or bone-in turkey breast
- 2 to 3 tablespoons water

1. Place the turkey breast in the Ninja Foodi PossibleCooker and add water. 2. Cover and cook on high for 2 to 4 hours, or on low for 4 to 9 hours, until the turkey is tender but not dry. 3. Turn the turkey over once during the cooking process. 4. For a browned finish, transfer the turkey to the oven and bake uncovered at 325ºF (165ºC) for 15 to 20 minutes after it's done in the Ninja Foodi PossibleCooker.

Chicken-Vegetable Dish

Prep time: 10 minutes | Cook time: 2 to 5 hours | Serves 4

- 4 skinless bone-in chicken breast halves
- 1 (15-ounce / 425-g) can crushed tomatoes
- 1 (10-ounce / 283-g) package frozen green beans
- 2 cups water or chicken broth
- 1 cup brown rice, uncooked
- 1 cup sliced mushrooms
- 2 carrots, chopped
- 1 onion, chopped
- ½ teaspoon minced garlic
- ½ teaspoon herb-blend seasoning
- ¼ teaspoon dried tarragon

1. In the Ninja Foodi PossibleCooker, mix all ingredients together thoroughly. 2. Cover and cook on high for 2 hours, then switch to low for an additional 3 to 5 hours.

Sweet Potato Chicken Shepherd's Pie

Prep time: 20 minutes | Cook time: 7¼ hours | Serves 2

- 2 medium sweet potatoes, peeled and cubed
- 2 tablespoons butter
- ¼ cup light cream
- ¾ teaspoon salt, divided
- 1 leek, white part only, chopped
- 2 garlic cloves, minced
- ½ teaspoon dried thyme leaves
- 2 carrots, sliced
- 2 celery stalks, sliced
- 5 boneless, skinless chicken thighs, cubed
- ¼ cup all-purpose flour
- ½ cup chicken stock
- 3 tablespoons tomato paste

1. In a medium saucepan over high heat, cover the sweet potatoes with water. Bring to a boil, and then reduce the heat to low and simmer for 20 to 25 minutes, or until the potatoes are tender. 2. Drain the potatoes and return them to the hot pot. Add the butter and mash the potatoes. Beat in the cream and ¼ teaspoon of salt and set aside. 3. In the Ninja Foodi PossibleCooker, combine the leek, garlic, carrots, and celery. 4. In a medium bowl, toss the chicken thighs with the flour and the remaining ½ teaspoon of salt, and add them to the Ninja Foodi PossibleCooker, stirring to combine. 5. In a small bowl, mix the stock, tomato paste, and thyme; pour the mixture into the Ninja Foodi PossibleCooker. 6. Spoon the mashed sweet potatoes on top of the chicken mixture. 7. Cover and cook on low for 6 to 7 hours, or until the chicken mixture is bubbly and the chicken registers 165°F (74°C) on a meat thermometer, and serve.

Roasted Red Pepper and Mozzarella Stuffed Chicken Breasts

Prep time: 15 minutes | Cook time: 6 to 8 hours | Serves 2

- 1 teaspoon extra-virgin olive oil
- 2 boneless, skinless chicken breasts
- ⅛ teaspoon sea salt
- Freshly ground black pepper
- 2 roasted red bell peppers, cut into thin strips
- 2 ounces (57 g) sliced mozzarella cheese
- ¼ cup roughly chopped fresh basil

1. Lightly coat the inside of the Ninja Foodi PossibleCooker with olive oil. 2. Take the chicken breasts and slice them horizontally, stopping just before cutting all the way through, creating a pocket. Season both sides with salt and pepper. 3. Layer roasted peppers inside each chicken breast half, then add slices of mozzarella cheese and sprinkle with fresh basil. Fold the chicken over to enclose the filling. 4. Carefully place the stuffed chicken breasts in the Ninja Foodi PossibleCooker, ensuring the filling stays inside. Cover and cook on low for 6 to 8 hours, or until the chicken is fully cooked.

Zesty Lemon Herb Chicken

Prep time: 20 minutes | Cook time: 3½ to 4½ hours | Serves 6

- 6 boneless, skinless chicken breast halves
- 1 teaspoon dried oregano
- ½ teaspoon seasoned salt
- ¼ teaspoon black pepper
- ¼ cup water
- 3 tablespoons lemon juice
- 2 garlic cloves, minced
- 2 teaspoons chicken bouillon granules
- 2 teaspoons fresh parsley, minced

1. Pat chicken dry with paper towels. 2. Combine oregano, seasoned salt, and pepper. Rub over chicken. 3. Brown chicken in a nonstick skillet over medium heat. 4. Place chicken in Ninja Foodi PossibleCooker. 5. Combine water, lemon juice, garlic, and bouillon in skillet. Bring to a boil, stirring to loosen browned bits. Pour over chicken. 6. Cover. Cook on low 3 to 4 hours. 7. Baste chicken. Add parsley. 8. Remove lid and cook 15 to 30 minutes longer, allowing juices to thicken slightly. 9. Serve.

Hungarian Chicken

Prep time: 10 minutes | Cook time: 7 to 8 hours | Serves 4

- 1 tablespoon extra-virgin olive oil
- 2 pounds (907 g) boneless chicken thighs
- ½ cup chicken broth
- Juice and zest of 1 lemon
- 2 teaspoons minced garlic
- 2 teaspoons paprika
- ¼ teaspoon salt
- 1 cup sour cream
- 1 tablespoon chopped parsley, for garnish

1. Grease the inside of the Ninja Foodi PossibleCooker insert with olive oil. 2. Arrange the chicken thighs in the insert. 3. In a separate bowl, mix the broth, lemon juice, lemon zest, garlic, paprika, and salt together. Pour this mixture over the chicken. 4. Cover and cook on low for 7 to 8 hours. 5. Once cooking is complete, turn off the heat and mix in the sour cream. 6. Serve the dish garnished with fresh parsley.

Tandoori-Style Chicken

Prep time: 10 minutes | Cook time: 4 to 8 hours | Serves 6

- 1 tablespoon freshly grated ginger
- 5 garlic cloves, minced
- 2 fresh green chiles, finely chopped
- ⅔ cup Greek yogurt
- 2 tablespoons mustard oil
- 1 tablespoon Kashmiri chili powder
- 1 tablespoon dried fenugreek leaves
- 1 tablespoon gram flour
- 2 teaspoons garam masala
- 1 teaspoon sea salt
- 1 teaspoon ground cumin
- Juice of 1 large lemon
- 1 whole chicken, about 3⅓ pounds (1½ kg)
- Handful fresh coriander leaves, chopped

1. Put the ginger, garlic, and green chiles in a spice grinder and grind to a paste. Empty into a large bowl and stir in all the other ingredients, except for the chicken and the coriander leaves. 2. Skin the chicken. Then, using a sharp knife, slash the chicken breasts and legs to allow the marinade to penetrate. 3. Marinate in the refrigerator for as long as you can leave it. (Overnight is fine.) 4. Preheat the Ninja Foodi PossibleCooker on high. My cooker has a stand I can sit meat on, but if you don't have one, scrunch up some foil and put it in the bottom of the cooker. Pour a few tablespoons of water in the bottom of the cooker and place the chicken on the foil. 5. Cook on high for 4 hours, or on low for 6 to 8 hours. 6. Remove the chicken from the cooker and cut it into pieces. Sprinkle the chopped coriander leaves over the chicken and serve.

Fruited Barbecue Chicken

Prep time: 5 minutes | Cook time: 4 hours | Serves 6 to 8

- 1 (29-ounce / 822-g) can tomato sauce
- 1 (20-ounce / 567-g) unsweetened crushed pineapple, undrained
- 2 tablespoons brown sugar
- 3 tablespoons vinegar
- 1 tablespoon instant minced onion
- 1 teaspoon paprika
- 2 teaspoons Worcestershire sauce
- ¼ teaspoon garlic powder
- ⅛ teaspoon pepper
- 3 pounds (1.4 kg) chicken, skinned and cubed
- 1 (11-ounce / 312-g) can mandarin oranges, drained

1. In the Ninja Foodi PossibleCooker, mix all ingredients except for the chicken and oranges. Add the chicken pieces. 2. Cover and cook on high for 4 hours. 3. Just before serving, fold in the oranges. Serve immediately.

Chicken Dijonaise

Prep time: 20 minutes | Cook time: 4 to 5 hours | Serves 8

- 3 to 4 pounds (1.4 to 1.8 kg) chicken parts (breasts, thighs, legs, or any combination), skin removed
- Salt and freshly ground black pepper
- 3 tablespoons extra-virgin olive oil
- 4 cloves garlic, minced
- 8 ounces (227 g) cipollini onions
- 1 pound (454 g) button mushrooms, cut in half if large
- 1 (16-ounce / 454-g) package frozen artichoke hearts, defrosted and quartered
- ½ cup dry white wine or vermouth
- 1½ cups chicken broth
- ⅔ cup Dijon mustard
- 1 bay leaf

1. Season the chicken with 1½ teaspoons of salt and ½ teaspoon of pepper. Heat oil in a large skillet over high heat and brown the chicken on all sides, working in batches if necessary. 2. Once browned, transfer the chicken to the insert of a 5- to 7-quart Ninja Foodi PossibleCooker. In the same skillet, add garlic and onions, sautéing until the onions begin to brown, about 4 minutes. 3. Stir in the mushrooms and cook until the liquid starts to evaporate, approximately 3 to 4 minutes. 4. Add the artichoke hearts and sauté for another 3 to 4 minutes until they are slightly browned. 5. Deglaze the skillet with wine, scraping up any browned bits from the bottom, then transfer everything to the Ninja Foodi PossibleCooker. In a separate bowl, whisk together the broth and mustard. 6. Pour the broth mixture into the Ninja Foodi PossibleCooker, add the bay leaf, and stir to combine. Cover and cook on low for 4 to 5 hours, until the chicken is tender. 7. Adjust seasoning with salt and pepper before serving.

Crispy Cereal-Coated Chicken

Prep time: 10 minutes | Cook time: 3½ to 4 hours | Serves 8

- 3½ pounds (1.6 kg) chicken pieces or whole chicken, cut up
- 2 cups skim milk
- 5 cups rice or corn cereal, finely crushed
- 1 teaspoon salt
- ½ teaspoon black pepper

1. Remove skin from chicken. Dip in milk. 2. Put crumbs in a plastic bag. Drop chicken pieces into bag to coat with cereal. Shake well. 3. Place chicken pieces in Ninja Foodi PossibleCooker. Sprinkle with salt and pepper. 4. Cover. Cook on high 3½ to 4 hours.

Chicken with Tropical Barbecue Sauce

Prep time: 5 minutes | Cook time: 3 to 9 hours | Serves 6

- ¼ cup molasses
- 2 tablespoons cider vinegar
- 2 tablespoons Worcestershire sauce
- 2 teaspoons prepared mustard
- ⅛ to ¼ teaspoon hot pepper sauce
- 2 tablespoons orange juice
- 3 whole chicken breasts, halved

1. In a bowl, mix together molasses, vinegar, Worcestershire sauce, mustard, hot pepper sauce, and orange juice. Brush this mixture over the chicken. 2. Place the chicken in the Ninja Foodi PossibleCooker. 3. Cover and cook on low for 7 to 9 hours, or on high for 3 to 4 hours.

Herb Turkey Breast

Prep time: 5 minutes | Cook time: 1 to 5 hours | Serves 6 to 8

- 1 (3- to 5-pound / 1.4- to 2.3-kg) bone-in turkey breast
- Salt and pepper to taste
- 2 carrots, cut in chunks
- 1 onion, cut in eighths
- 2 ribs celery, cut in chunks

1. Rinse turkey breast and pat dry. Season well inside with salt. 2. Place vegetables in bottom of Ninja Foodi PossibleCooker. Sprinkle with pepper. Place turkey breast on top of vegetables. 3. Cover and cook on high 1 to 3 hours, on low 4 to 5 hours, or until tender but not dry or mushy.

Turkey with Mushroom Sauce

Prep time: 15 minutes | Cook time: 7 to 8 hours | Serves 12

- 1 large boneless, skinless turkey breast, halved
- 2 tablespoons butter, melted
- 2 tablespoons dried parsley
- ½ teaspoon dried oregano
- ½ teaspoon salt
- ¼ teaspoon black pepper
- ½ cup white wine
- 1 cup sliced fresh mushrooms
- 2 tablespoons cornstarch
- ¼ cup cold water

1. Place turkey in Ninja Foodi PossibleCooker. Brush with butter. 2. Mix together parsley, oregano, salt, pepper, and wine. Pour over turkey. 3. Top with mushrooms. 4. Cover. Cook on low 7 to 8 hours. 5. Remove turkey and keep warm. 6. Skim any fat from cooking juices. 7. In a saucepan, combine cornstarch and water until smooth. Gradually add cooking juices. Bring to a boil. Cook and stir 2 minutes until thickened. 8. Slice turkey and serve with sauce.

Chicken and Shrimp Jambalaya

Prep time: 15 minutes | Cook time: 2¼ to 3¾ hours | Serves 5 to 6

- 1 (3½- to 4-pound / 1.6- to 1.8-kg) roasting chicken, cut up
- 3 onions, diced
- 1 carrot, sliced
- 3 to 4 garlic cloves, minced
- 1 teaspoon dried oregano
- 1 teaspoon dried basil
- 1 teaspoon salt
- ⅛ teaspoon white pepper
- 1 (14-ounce / 397-g) crushed tomatoes
- 1 pound (454 g) shelled raw shrimp
- 2 cups rice, cooked

1. In the Ninja Foodi PossibleCooker, mix all ingredients except for the shrimp and rice. 2. Cover and cook on low for 2 to 3½ hours, or until the chicken is tender. 3. Stir in the shrimp and rice. 4. Cover and cook on high for an additional 15 to 20 minutes, or until the shrimp are cooked through.

One-Pot Herb Chicken Dinner

Prep time: 30 minutes | Cook time: 6 hours | Serves 6

- 6 to 8 potatoes, quartered
- 1 to 2 large onions, sliced
- 3 to 5 carrots, cubed
- 1 (5-pound / 2.3-kg) chicken, skin removed
- 1 small onion, chopped
- 1 teaspoon black pepper
- 1 tablespoon whole cloves
- 1 tablespoon garlic salt
- 1 tablespoon chopped fresh oregano
- 1 teaspoon dried rosemary
- ½ cup lemon juice or chicken broth

1. Layer potatoes, sliced onions, and carrots in bottom of Ninja Foodi PossibleCooker. 2. Rinse and pat chicken dry. In bowl mix together chopped onions, pepper, cloves, and garlic salt. Dredge chicken in seasonings. Place in cooker over vegetables. Spoon any remaining seasonings over chicken. 3. Sprinkle with oregano and rosemary. Pour lemon juice over chicken. 4. Cover. Cook on low 6 hours.

Creamy Italian Chicken

Prep time: 10 minutes | Cook time: 4 hours | Serves 4

- 4 boneless, skinless chicken breast halves
- 1 envelope dry Italian salad dressing mix
- ¼ cup water
- 1 (8-ounce / 227-g) package cream cheese, softened
- 1 (10¾-ounce / 305-g) can cream of chicken or celery soup
- 1 (4-ounce / 113-g) can mushroom stems and pieces, drained (optional)

1. Place the chicken in the Ninja Foodi PossibleCooker. In a separate bowl, mix the salad dressing and water, then pour over the chicken. 2. Cover and cook on low for 3 hours. 3. In another bowl, beat together the cream cheese and soup until smooth. If desired, stir in mushrooms. Pour this mixture over the chicken. 4. Cover and cook on low for an additional hour, or until the chicken is tender but not dry.

Barbecued Turkey

Prep time: 15 minutes | Cook time: 3 to 4 hours | Serves 6

- 3 large onions, coarsely chopped
- 2 red bell peppers, seeded and coarsely chopped
- 1 (4-pound / 1.8-kg) bone-in turkey breast, skin removed
- 1 cup ketchup
- 1 cup tomato sauce
- ½ cup Dijon mustard
- ¼ cup firmly packed light brown sugar
- 2 tablespoons Worcestershire sauce
- ½ teaspoon Tabasco sauce

1. Put the onions and bell peppers in the bottom of an insert of a 5- to 7-quart Ninja Foodi PossibleCooker. Put the turkey breast on top of the vegetables. Stir the ketchup, tomato sauce, mustard, sugar, Worcestershire, and Tabasco in a small mixing bowl to combine. 2. Brush some of the barbecue sauce on the turkey breast, then pour the rest in the slow-cooker insert. Cover and cook on high for 3 to 4 hours, until the turkey is cooked and registers 175°F (79°C) on an instant-read thermometer. 3. Carefully remove the turkey from the Ninja Foodi PossibleCooker, cover with aluminum foil, and allow to rest for 20 minutes before carving. 4. Strain the sauce through a fine-mesh sieve into a bowl, discarding the solids. Return the sauce to the Ninja Foodi PossibleCooker. 5. Carve the turkey and serve with the sauce or return the turkey to the Ninja Foodi PossibleCooker with the sauce and serve from the cooker set on warm.

Chicken Mole

Prep time: 15 minutes | Cook time: 7 to 8 hours | Serves 6

- 3 tablespoons extra-virgin olive oil or ghee, divided
- 2 pounds (907 g) boneless chicken thighs and breasts
- Salt, for seasoning
- Freshly ground black pepper, for seasoning
- 1 sweet onion, chopped
- 1 tablespoon minced garlic
- 1 (28 ounces / 794 g) can diced tomatoes
- 4 dried chile peppers, soaked
- in water for 2 hours and chopped
- 3 ounces (85 g) dark chocolate, chopped
- ¼ cup natural peanut butter
- 1½ teaspoons ground cumin
- ¾ teaspoon ground cinnamon
- ½ teaspoon chili powder
- ½ cup coconut cream
- 2 tablespoons chopped cilantro, for garnish

1. Lightly grease the insert of the Ninja Foodi PossibleCooker with 1 tablespoon of the olive oil. 2. In a large skillet over medium-high heat, heat the remaining 2 tablespoons of the olive oil. 3. Lightly season the chicken with salt and pepper, add to the skillet, and brown for about 5 minutes, turning once. 4. Add the onion and garlic and sauté for an additional 3 minutes. 5. Transfer the chicken, onion, and garlic to the Ninja Foodi PossibleCooker, and stir in the tomatoes, chiles, chocolate, peanut butter, cumin, cinnamon, and chili powder. 6. Cover and cook on low for 7 to 8 hours. 7. Stir in the coconut cream, and serve hot, topped with the cilantro.

Another Chicken in a Pot

Prep time: 10 minutes | Cook time: 3½ to 10 hours | Serves 4 to 6

- 1 (1-pound / 454-g) bag baby carrots
- 1 small onion, diced
- 1 (14½-ounce / 411-g) can green beans
- 1 (3-pound / 1.4-kg) whole chicken, cut into serving-
- size pieces
- 2 teaspoons salt
- ½ teaspoon black pepper
- ½ cup chicken broth
- ¼ cup white wine
- ½ to 1 teaspoon dried basil

1. Layer the bottom of the Ninja Foodi PossibleCooker with sliced carrots, diced onion, and beans. Place the chicken on top. Season with salt and pepper, then pour in the broth and wine. Finish by sprinkling with fresh basil. 2. Cover the Ninja Foodi PossibleCooker and cook on low for 8 to 10 hours, or on high for 3½ to 5 hours, until the chicken is tender and fully cooked.

Chicken with Mango Chutney

Prep time: 10 minutes | Cook time: 6 to 8 hours | Serves 2

- 12 ounces (340 g) boneless, skinless chicken thighs, cut into 1-inch pieces
- ½ cup thinly sliced red onion
- 1 cup canned mango or peaches, drained and diced
- 2 tablespoons golden raisins
- 2 tablespoons apple cider vinegar
- 1 teaspoon minced fresh ginger
- ¼ teaspoon red pepper flakes
- 1 teaspoon curry powder
- ¼ teaspoon ground cinnamon
- ⅛ teaspoon sea salt

1. Put all the ingredients to the Ninja Foodi PossibleCooker and gently stir to combine. 2. Cover and cook on low for 6 to 8 hours. The chutney should be thick and sweet and the chicken tender and cooked through.

Chicken and Bean Torta

Prep time: 20 minutes | Cook time: 4 to 5 hours | Serves 6

- 1 pound (454 g) uncooked boneless, skinless chicken breasts
- 1 medium onion
- ½ teaspoon garlic salt
- ¼ teaspoon black pepper
- 1 (15-ounce / 425-g) can ranch-style black beans
- 1 (15-ounce / 425-g) can low-sodium diced tomatoes
- with green chilies
- 4 tortillas
- 1½ cups shredded low-fat Cheddar cheese
- Salsa
- Fat-free sour cream
- Lettuce
- Tomatoes
- Nonfat cooking spray

1. Begin by cutting the chicken into bite-sized pieces and browning them along with diced onion in a nonstick skillet. Once browned, drain off any excess fat. 2. Season the mixture with garlic salt and pepper, then stir in the drained beans and diced tomatoes until well combined. 3. Create an X with strips of aluminum foil in the bottom of the Ninja Foodi PossibleCooker, extending the edges up the sides. Lightly coat the foil and the cooker with nonfat cooking spray to prevent sticking. 4. Place a tortilla at the bottom of the Ninja Foodi PossibleCooker, followed by a layer of the chicken mixture and a sprinkle of cheese. 5. Repeat the layering process two more times, finishing with a tortilla on top and an extra layer of cheese. 6. Cover the Ninja Foodi PossibleCooker and set it to low, cooking for 4 to 5 hours until heated through and melty. 7. Once finished, use the foil edges to carefully lift the layered dish onto a serving platter. Gently peel away the foil and discard. 8. Serve hot,

accompanied by salsa, sour cream, fresh lettuce, and diced tomatoes for added flavor and texture.

Herb-Infused BBQ Chicken

Prep time: 10 minutes | Cook time: 6 to 8 hours | Serves 4 to 6

- 1 whole chicken, cut up, or 8 of your favorite pieces
- 1 onion, thinly sliced
- 1 bottle Sweet Baby Ray's
- Barbecue Sauce
- 1 teaspoon dried oregano
- 1 teaspoon dried basil

1. Place chicken in Ninja Foodi PossibleCooker. 2. Mix onion slices, sauce, oregano, and basil together in a bowl. Pour over chicken, covering as well as possible. 3. Cover and cook on low 6 to 8 hours, or until chicken is tender but not dry.

Come-Back-for-More Barbecued Chicken

Prep time: 10 minutes | Cook time: 6 to 8 hours | Serves 6 to 8

- 6 to 8 chicken breast halves
- 1 cup ketchup
- ⅓ cup Worcestershire sauce
- ½ cup brown sugar
- 1 teaspoon chili powder
- ½ cup water

1. Arrange the chicken in the Ninja Foodi PossibleCooker. 2. In a sizable bowl, combine the rest of the ingredients by whisking until well blended. Pour the sauce over the chicken. 3. Secure the lid and set the cooker to low, allowing it to simmer for 6 to 8 hours, or until the chicken is perfectly tender without being overdone.

Loretta's Hot Chicken

Prep time: 15 minutes | Cook time: 2 hours | Serves 12

- 8 cups cubed cooked chicken or turkey
- 1 medium onion, chopped
- 1 cup chopped celery
- 2 cups mayonnaise
- 1 cup cubed American cheese

1. In the Ninja Foodi PossibleCooker, mix together all ingredients except for the buns. 2. Cover and cook on high for 2 hours. 3. Serve hot.

Curried Chicken Divan Bake

Prep time: 15 minutes | Cook time: 3 hours | Serves 6

- 4 tablespoons (½ stick) unsalted butter
- 1½ teaspoons curry powder
- ¼ cup all-purpose flour
- 2 cups chicken broth
- 1 cup evaporated milk
- 8 chicken breast halves, skin and bones removed
- 1½ cups finely shredded sharp Cheddar cheese

1. Melt the butter in a saucepan over medium-high heat. Add the curry powder and sauté for 30 seconds. 2. Add the flour and cook for 3 minutes, whisking constantly. Add the broth and bring to the mixture to a boil. Add the milk and remove the sauce from the heat and allow to cool. 3. Place the chicken in the insert of a 5- to 7-quart Ninja Foodi PossibleCooker, stacking evenly. Pour the cooled sauce over the chicken. Cover and cook on high for 3 hours. 4. Sprinkle the cheese over the chicken, cover, and cook for an additional 1 hour, until the chicken is cooked through. 5. Serve the chicken from the cooker set on warm.

Punjabi Chicken Curry

Prep time: 20 minutes | Cook time: 4 to 6 hours | Serves 6

- 2 tablespoons vegetable oil
- 3 onions, finely diced
- 6 garlic cloves, finely chopped
- 1 heaped tablespoon freshly grated ginger
- 1 (14-ounce / 397-g) can plum tomatoes
- 1 teaspoon salt
- 1 teaspoon turmeric
- 1 teaspoon chili powder
- Handful coriander stems, finely chopped
- 3 fresh green chiles, finely chopped
- 12 pieces chicken, mixed thighs and drumsticks, or a whole chicken, skinned, trimmed, and chopped
- 2 teaspoons garam masala
- Handful fresh coriander leaves, chopped

1. Heat the oil in a frying pan (or in the Ninja Foodi PossibleCooker if you have a sear setting). Add the diced onions and cook for 5 minutes. Add the garlic and continue to cook for 10 minutes until the onions are brown. 2. Heat the Ninja Foodi PossibleCooker to high and add the onion-and-garlic mixture. Stir in the ginger, tomatoes, salt, turmeric, chili powder, coriander stems, and chiles. 3. Add the chicken pieces. Cover and cook on low for 6 hours, or on high for 4 hours. 4. Once cooked, check the seasoning, and then stir in the garam masala and coriander leaves.

Cape Breton Chicken

Prep time: 15 minutes | Cook time: 7 hours | Serves 5

- 4 boneless, skinless chicken breast halves, uncooked, cubed
- 1 medium onion, chopped
- 1 medium green bell pepper, chopped
- 1 cup chopped celery
- 1 quart low-sodium stewed
- or crushed tomatoes
- 1 cup water
- ½ cup tomato paste
- 2 tablespoons Worcestershire sauce
- 2 tablespoons brown sugar
- 1 teaspoon black pepper

1. Add all ingredients to the Ninja Foodi PossibleCooker. 2. Secure the lid in place. Let it cook on low for 7 hours. 3. Dish out and enjoy your meal.

Moroccan Chicken with Apricots, Almonds, and Olives

Prep time: 20 minutes | Cook time: 3 hours | Serves 4

- 3 pounds (1.4 kg) skinless chicken thighs
- 1 yellow onion, cut into ½-inch wedges
- 1 teaspoon ground cumin
- ½ teaspoon ground ginger
- ½ teaspoon ground coriander
- ¼ teaspoon ground cinnamon
- ¼ teaspoon cayenne pepper
- Sea salt
- Black pepper
- 1 bay leaf
- ⅓ cup chicken stock
- 1 (15-ounce / 425-g) can chickpeas, drained and rinsed
- ½ cup green olives
- ½ cup dried Turkish apricots
- ⅓ cup sliced almonds, toasted

1. In a large bowl, combine the chicken thighs and onion. Add cumin, coriander, ginger, cinnamon, and cayenne, then toss to coat. Season with salt and pepper. 2. Transfer the mixture to the Ninja Foodi PossibleCooker and add the bay leaf along with the chicken stock. 3. Cover and cook on high for 2 hours. 4. Stir in the chickpeas, olives, and apricots. Cover and cook for an additional hour, until the chicken is tender and the apricots are plump. 5. Discard the bay leaf and adjust seasoning with salt and pepper. 6. Preheat the oven to 350ºF (180ºC). Spread almonds in a pie plate and toast for about 7 minutes, until fragrant and lightly golden, watching carefully to prevent burning. 7. Serve the hot chicken and vegetables in shallow bowls, topped with toasted almonds.

Chicken Tortilla Casserole

Prep time: 25 minutes | Cook time: 3 to 6 hours | Serves 8 to 10

- 4 whole boneless, skinless chicken breasts, cooked and cut in 1-inch pieces (reserve ¼ cup broth chicken was cooked in)
- 10 (6-inch) flour tortillas, cut in strips about ½-inch wide × 2-inches long
- 2 medium onions, chopped
- 1 teaspoon canola oil
- 1 (10¾-ounce / 305-g) can fat-free chicken broth
- 1 (10¾-ounce / 305-g) can 98% fat-free cream of mushroom soup
- 2 (4-ounce / 113-g) cans mild green chilies, chopped
- 1 egg
- 1 cup shredded low-fat Cheddar cheese

1. Pour reserved chicken broth in Ninja Foodi PossibleCooker sprayed with nonfat cooking spray. 2. Scatter half the tortilla strips in bottom of Ninja Foodi PossibleCooker. 3. Mix remaining ingredients together, except the second half of the tortilla strips and the cheese. 4. Layer half the chicken mixture into the cooker, followed by the other half of the tortillas, followed by the rest of the chicken mix. 5. Cover. Cook on low 4 to 6 hours, or on high 3 to 5 hours. 6. Add the cheese to the top of the dish during the last 20 to 30 minutes of cooking. 7. Uncover and allow casserole to rest 15 minutes before serving.

Chicken Cacciatore with Porcini and Cremini Mushrooms

Prep time: 15 minutes | Cook time: 4 to 5 hours | Serves 6 to 8

- 4 tablespoons extra-virgin olive oil
- 1 pound (454 g) cremini mushrooms, quartered
- 2 teaspoons salt
- Pinch red pepper flakes
- 1 teaspoon dried oregano
- 3 cloves garlic, minced
- ¼ cup dried porcini mushrooms, crumbled
- ¼ cup red wine
- 1 (28- to 32-ounce / 794- to 907-g) can crushed tomatoes, with their juice
- 10 chicken thighs, skin and bones removed

1. In a large skillet, heat 2 tablespoons of oil over high heat. Add mushrooms, 1 teaspoon of salt, red pepper flakes, oregano, and garlic, then sauté until the liquid evaporates, about 7 to 10 minutes. 2. Soak the porcinis in a small bowl with wine to soften. Once ready, add the porcinis and wine mixture along with the tomatoes to the skillet. 3. Pour the mixture from the pan into the insert of a 5- to 7-quart Ninja Foodi PossibleCooker. 4. Season the chicken with the remaining 1 teaspoon of salt. In the same skillet, heat the other 2 tablespoons of oil over high heat, then add the chicken and brown it on all sides for 15 to 20 minutes. 5. Place the browned chicken into the Ninja Foodi PossibleCooker, ensuring it's submerged in the sauce. Cover and cook on low for 4 to 5 hours until the chicken is tender and fully cooked, skimming off any excess fat from the sauce. 6. Keep the cooker on warm and serve directly from it.

Savory Chicken

Prep time: 15 minutes | Cook time: 8 to 10 hours | Serves 4

- 2½ pounds (1.1 kg) chicken pieces, skinned
- 1 pound (454 g) fresh tomatoes, chopped, or 1 (15-ounce / 425-g) can stewed tomatoes
- 2 tablespoons white wine
- 1 bay leaf
- ¼ teaspoon pepper
- 2 garlic cloves, minced
- 1 onion, chopped
- ½ cup chicken broth
- 1 teaspoon dried thyme
- 1½ teaspoons salt
- 2 cups broccoli, cut into bite-sized pieces

1. In the Ninja Foodi PossibleCooker, mix all ingredients except for the broccoli. 2. Cover and cook on low for 8 to 10 hours. 3. Add the broccoli 30 minutes before serving.

Reuben-Style Chicken Casserole

Prep time: 30 minutes | Cook time: 4 hours | Serves 6

- 2 (16-ounce / 454-g) cans sauerkraut, rinsed and drained, divided
- 1 cup Light Russian salad dressing, divided
- 6 boneless, skinless chicken
- breast halves, divided
- 1 tablespoon prepared mustard, divided
- 6 slices Swiss cheese
- Fresh parsley for garnish (optional)

1. Place half the sauerkraut in the Ninja Foodi PossibleCooker. Drizzle with ⅓ cup dressing. 2. Top with 3 chicken breast halves. Spread half the mustard on top of the chicken. 3. Top with remaining sauerkraut and chicken breasts. Drizzle with another ⅓ cup dressing. (Save the remaining dressing until serving time.) 4. Cover and cook on low for 4 hours, or until the chicken is tender, but not dry or mushy. 5. To serve, place a breast half on each of 6 plates. Divide the sauerkraut over the chicken. Top each with a slice of cheese and a drizzle of the remaining dressing. Garnish with parsley if you wish, just before serving.

Shredded Chicken Chili Tacos

Prep time: 15 minutes | Cook time: 4 hours | Serves 4

- 2 pounds (907 g) boneless, skinless chicken thighs (about 6)
- 4 garlic cloves, thinly sliced
- ½ cup mild or medium salsa, plus more for serving
- 2 to 2 tablespoons chopped chipotle chiles in adobo sauce
- 1 tablespoon chili powder
- Coarse salt and freshly ground pepper
- 8 taco shells or tortillas
- Grated cheddar cheese, sour cream, chopped avocado, fresh cilantro, and lime wedges, for serving

1. Preheat a 5- to 6-quart Ninja Foodi PossibleCooker. 2. Combine chicken, garlic, salsa, chiles, chili powder, 1 teaspoon salt, and ¼ teaspoon pepper in the Ninja Foodi PossibleCooker. Cover and cook on high until chicken is cooked through, 4 hours (or on low for 8 hours). 3. Transfer chicken to a bowl. Using two forks, shred chicken; moisten with cooking liquid. Season with salt and pepper. Serve in taco shells, with cheese, sour cream, avocado, cilantro, lime wedges, and salsa.

Low-Fat Chicken Cacciatore

Prep time: 15 minutes | Cook time: 8 hours | Serves 10

- 2 pounds (907 g) uncooked boneless, skinless chicken breasts, cubed
- ½ pound (227 g) fresh mushrooms
- 1 bell pepper, chopped
- 1 medium-sized onion, chopped
- 1 (12-ounce / 340-g) can low-sodium chopped tomatoes
- 1 (6-ounce / 170-g) can low-sodium tomato paste
- 1 (12-ounce / 340-g) can low-sodium tomato sauce
- ½ teaspoon dried oregano
- ½ teaspoon dried basil
- ½ teaspoon garlic powder
- ½ teaspoon salt
- ½ teaspoon black pepper

1. Combine all ingredients in Ninja Foodi PossibleCooker. 2. Cover. Cook on low 8 hours. 3. Serve.

Maple-Glazed Turkey Breast with Rice

Prep time: 15 minutes | Cook time: 4 to 6 hours | Serves 4

- 1 (6-ounce / 170-g) package long-grain wild rice mix
- 1½ cups water
- 1 (2-pound / 907-g) boneless turkey breast, cut into 1½ to 2-inch chunks
- ¼ cup maple syrup
- 1 onion, chopped
- ¼ teaspoon ground cinnamon
- ½ teaspoon salt (optional)

1. Add all the ingredients into the Ninja Foodi PossibleCooker. 2. Set it to cook on low for 4 to 6 hours, until the turkey and rice are tender but still retain their texture, avoiding any dryness or mushiness.

Chicken Breasts with Cornbread Stuffing

Prep time: 30 minutes | Cook time: 2½ to 3 hours | Serves 6

- 6 chicken breast halves, skinned and boned
- 1½ teaspoons salt
- ⅛ teaspoon cayenne pepper
- 2 tablespoons unsalted butter
- ½ cup finely chopped sweet onion, such as Vidalia (about ½ medium onion)
- 1 jalapeño pepper, seeded and finely chopped
- ½ cup finely chopped red bell pepper
- 1 cup frozen white corn, defrosted and drained
- 1 package Jiffy cornbread mix
- ¼ cup sour cream
- ½ cup mayonnaise
- 2 tablespoons olive oil
- 1 medium onion, chopped
- 1 teaspoon ground cumin
- ½ teaspoon dried oregano
- 2½ cups chicken broth
- 2 tablespoons cornstarch
- 1 cup heavy cream
- 1 cup finely shredded mild Cheddar cheese
- ½ cup finely chopped fresh cilantro

1. Place the chicken, skin-side down, between two sheets of plastic wrap and pound it until it's an even thickness. 2. Season the chicken with salt and cayenne. In a small skillet over medium-high heat, melt the butter, then add the sweet onion, jalapeño, and bell pepper. Sauté for about 4 minutes until the onion softens. 3. Transfer the sautéed vegetables to a mixing bowl to cool. Once cooled, mix in the corn, cornbread mix, sour cream, and mayonnaise until the mixture is thick. Spread this filling over the chicken breasts, then roll the chicken tightly from the top, tucking in the sides, and secure with 4-inch skewers, silicone loops, or kitchen twine. 4. Place the rolled chicken in the insert of a 5- to 7-quart Ninja Foodi PossibleCooker, arranging it in a single layer. In the same skillet, heat oil over medium-high heat, then add onion, cumin, and oregano, sautéing for about 3 minutes until the onion is soft. Pour this mixture into the Ninja Foodi PossibleCooker and add the broth. 5. Cover and cook on high for 2½ to 3 hours, until the chicken reaches an internal temperature of 170°F (77°C). Carefully move the chicken to a serving platter and cover it with aluminum foil. Pour the cooking sauce into a saucepan and bring to a boil, reducing it by half. 6. In a small bowl, mix cornstarch with cream, then whisk it into the sauce. Boil while whisking until thickened. Remove from heat and stir in cheese and cilantro until melted. Taste and adjust seasoning as needed. 7. Take out the skewers, silicone loops, or kitchen twine. Using a serrated knife, slice each chicken breast diagonally into four pieces and serve atop the sauce, with extra sauce on the side.

Chapter 6

Stews and Soups

Chapter 6 Stews and Soups

Crab and Vegetable Soup

Prep time: 20 minutes | Cook time: 8 to 10 hours | Serves 10

- 1 pound (454 g) carrots, sliced
- ½ bunch celery, sliced
- 1 large onion, diced
- 2 (10-ounce / 283-g) bags frozen mixed vegetables, or your choice of frozen vegetables
- 1 (12-ounce / 340-g) can tomato juice
- 1 pound (454 g) ham, cubed
- 1 pound (454 g) beef, cubed
- 6 slices bacon, chopped
- 1 teaspoon salt
- ¼ teaspoon pepper
- 1 tablespoon Old Bay seasoning
- 1 pound (454 g) claw crab meat

1. Combine all ingredients except seasonings and crab meat in large Ninja Foodi PossibleCooker. Pour in water until cooker is half-full. 2. Add spices. Stir in thoroughly. Put crab on top. 3. Cover. Cook on low 8 to 10 hours. 4. Stir well and serve.

Mushroom-Beef Stew

Prep time: 20 minutes | Cook time: 6 to 7½ hours | Serves 8 to 10

- 1 pound (454 g) sirloin, cubed
- 2 tablespoons flour
- Oil
- 1 large onion, chopped
- 2 garlic cloves, minced
- ½ pound (227 g) button mushrooms, sliced
- 2 ribs celery, sliced
- 2 carrots, sliced
- 3 to 4 large potatoes, cubed
- 2 teaspoons seasoned salt
- 1 (14½-ounce / 411-g) can beef stock, or 2 bouillon cubes dissolved in 1⅔ cups water
- ½ to 1 cup good red wine

1. Coat the sirloin with flour and sear it in a skillet until browned, then set aside the drippings. Place the meat into the Ninja Foodi PossibleCooker. 2. In the reserved drippings, sauté the onion, garlic, and mushrooms until they're softened. Add this mixture to the meat in the Ninja Foodi PossibleCooker. 3. Incorporate all the remaining ingredients into the cooker. 4. Cover and cook on low for 6 hours.

Check if the vegetables are tender; if they need more time, continue cooking on low for an additional 1 to 1½ hours. 5. Serve hot.

Chet's Hearty Trucker Stew

Prep time: 15 minutes | Cook time: 2 to 3 hours | Serves 8

- 1 pound (454 g) bulk pork sausage, cooked and drained
- 1 pound (454 g) ground beef, cooked and drained
- 1 (31-ounce / 879-g) can pork and beans
- 1 (16-ounce / 454-g) can light kidney beans
- 1 (16-ounce / 454-g) can
- dark kidney beans
- 1 (14½-ounce / 411-g) can waxed beans, drained
- 1 (14½-ounce / 411-g) can lima beans, drained
- 1 cup ketchup
- 1 cup brown sugar
- 1 tablespoon spicy prepared mustard

1. Combine all ingredients in Ninja Foodi PossibleCooker. 2. Cover. Simmer on high 2 to 3 hours.

Chili, Chicken, Corn Chowder

Prep time: 15 minutes | Cook time: 4 hours | Serves 6 to 8

- ¼ cup oil
- 1 large onion, diced
- 1 garlic clove, minced
- 1 rib celery, finely chopped
- 2 cups frozen or canned corn
- 2 cups cooked chicken, deboned and cubed
- 1 (4-ounce / 113-g) can diced green chilies
- ½ teaspoon black pepper
- 2 cups chicken broth
- Salt to taste
- 1 cup half-and-half

1. In a saucepan, heat oil and sauté the onion, garlic, and celery until they are soft. 2. Add the corn, chicken, and chilies, and sauté for another 2 to 3 minutes. 3. Transfer all ingredients, except for the half-and-half, into the Ninja Foodi PossibleCooker. 4. Cover the Ninja Foodi PossibleCooker and cook on low for 4 hours. 5. Before serving, stir in the half-and-half, ensuring it's heated through without bringing it to a boil.

Polish Sausage and Sauerkraut Stew

Prep time: 15 minutes | Cook time: 4 to 8 hours | Serves 6 to 8

- 1 (10¾-ounce / 305-g) can cream of celery soup
- ⅓ cup packed brown sugar
- 1 (27-ounce / 765-g) can sauerkraut, drained
- 1½ pounds (680 g) Polish

- sausage, cut into 2-inch pieces and browned
- 4 medium potatoes, cubed
- 1 cup chopped onions
- 1 cup shredded Monterey Jack cheese

1. Combine soup, sugar, and sauerkraut. Stir in sausage, potatoes, and onions. 2. Cover. Cook on low 8 hours, or on high 4 hours. 3. Stir in cheese and serve.

Mediterranean Beef Stew with Rosemary and Balsamic Vinegar

Prep time: 20 minutes | Cook time: 6 to 8 hours | Serves 6

- 8 ounces (227 g) mushrooms, sliced
- 1 large yellow onion, diced
- 2 tablespoons olive oil
- 2 pounds (907 g) chuck steak, trimmed and cut into bite-size pieces
- 1 cup beef stock
- 1 (15-ounce / 425-g) can diced tomatoes, with the juice
- ½ cup tomato sauce
- ¼ cup balsamic vinegar

- 1 (5-ounce / 142-g) can chopped black olives
- ½ cup thinly sliced garlic cloves
- 2 tablespoons finely chopped fresh rosemary (or 1 tablespoon dried rosemary)
- 2 tablespoons finely chopped fresh flat-leaf parsley (or 1 tablespoon dried parsley)
- 2 tablespoons capers, drained
- Sea salt
- Black pepper

1. Add the mushrooms and onion to the Ninja Foodi PossibleCooker. 2. In a large skillet over medium-high heat, warm the olive oil. Once hot, add the beef and cook, stirring frequently, for 10 to 15 minutes until it's nicely browned. If the beef browns too quickly, reduce the heat to medium. Transfer the browned beef to the Ninja Foodi PossibleCooker. 3. Pour the beef stock into the skillet and let it simmer for 5 minutes, scraping the tasty brown bits from the bottom with a wooden spoon. Pour this stock into the Ninja Foodi PossibleCooker. 4. In the Ninja Foodi PossibleCooker, mix in the diced tomatoes, tomato sauce, vinegar, olives, garlic, rosemary, parsley, and capers. Season with salt and pepper, then stir gently to combine. Cover and cook on low for 6 to 8 hours (you can use high for 3 to 4 hours, but low yields better results). Adjust seasoning with more salt and pepper if needed, and serve warm.

Aunt Thelma's Homemade Soup

Prep time: 15 minutes | Cook time: 4½ hours | Serves 10 to 12

- 7 cups water
- 4 chicken or vegetable bouillon cubes
- 1 cup thinly sliced carrots
- 1 (1-pound / 454-g) package frozen peas
- 1 (1-pound / 454-g) package frozen corn
- 1 (1-pound / 454-g) package frozen lima beans
- 1 bay leaf

- ¼ teaspoon dill seed
- 1 (28-ounce / 794-g) can whole tomatoes
- 1 cup diced raw potatoes
- 1 cup chopped onions
- 2 to 3 teaspoons salt
- ½ teaspoon dried basil
- ¼ teaspoon pepper
- 2 tablespoons cornstarch
- ¼ cup cold water

1. In the Ninja Foodi PossibleCooker, mix all ingredients except for the cornstarch and ¼ cup of water. 2. Cover the cooker and let it simmer on high for 4 hours, or until the vegetables are tender. 3. About 30 minutes before the cooking time is up, combine the cornstarch with the cold water in a bowl until smooth. Take out 1 cup of broth from the cooker and mix it with the cornstarch mixture. Once smooth, stir this back into the soup. Cover and cook for an additional 30 minutes. 4. Serve hot.

Hearty Vegetable Soup

Prep time: 20 minutes | Cook time: 8 to 10 hours | Serves 8 to 10

- 1 pound (454 g) ground beef, browned
- 1 cup chopped onions
- 1 (15-ounce / 425-g) can kidney beans or butter beans, undrained
- 1 cup sliced carrots
- ¼ cup rice, uncooked

- 1 quart stewed tomatoes
- 3½ cups water
- 5 beef bouillon cubes
- 1 tablespoon parsley flakes
- 1 teaspoon salt
- ⅛ teaspoon pepper
- ¼ teaspoon dried basil
- 1 bay leaf

1. Combine all ingredients in Ninja Foodi PossibleCooker. 2. Cover. Cook on low 8 to 10 hours.

Mango and Coconut Chicken Soup

Prep time: 25 minutes | Cook time: 6 hours | Serves 6

- 1 (3- to 4-pound / 1.4- to 1.8-kg) broiler/fryer chicken, skin removed and cut up
- 2 tablespoons canola oil
- 1 (15-ounce / 425-g) can whole baby corn, drained
- 1 (10-ounce / 283-g) package frozen chopped spinach, thawed
- 1 cup frozen shelled edamame, thawed
- 1 small sweet red pepper, chopped
- 1 can (13.6-ounce / 386-g) light coconut milk
- ½ cup mango salsa
- 1 teaspoon minced fresh ginger root
- 1 medium mango, peeled and chopped
- 2 tablespoons lime juice
- 2 green onions, chopped

1. In a large skillet, heat oil and brown the chicken in batches. Once browned, transfer the chicken and any drippings to a 5-quart Ninja Foodi PossibleCooker. Add the corn, spinach, edamame, and pepper. In a separate bowl, mix the coconut milk, salsa, and ginger, then pour this over the vegetables. 2. Cover the Ninja Foodi PossibleCooker and cook on low for 6 to 8 hours, until the chicken is tender. Remove the chicken and let it cool slightly. When it's cool enough to handle, take the meat off the bones and cut or shred it into bite-sized pieces before returning it to the Ninja Foodi PossibleCooker. 3. Just before serving, mix in the mango and lime juice, and top with green onions.

Fajita Stew

Prep time: 15 minutes | Cook time: 6½ to 8½ hours | Serves 8

- 2½ pounds (1.1 kg) boneless beef top round steak
- 1 onion, chopped
- 1 (1-ounce / 28-g) envelope dry fajita seasoning mix (about 2 tablespoons)
- 1 (14-ounce / 397-g) diced tomatoes, undrained
- 1 red bell pepper, cut into 1-inch pieces
- ¼ cup flour
- ¼ cup water

1. Remove any excess fat from the beef and cut it into 2-inch pieces. Place the beef in the Ninja Foodi PossibleCooker along with the onion. 2. In a separate bowl, combine the fajita seasoning with the undrained tomatoes, then pour this mixture over the beef. 3. Layer the chopped peppers on top of the beef mixture. 4. Cover the Ninja Foodi PossibleCooker and cook on low for 6 to 8 hours, or

until the beef is tender. 5. In a small bowl, mix the flour and water until well combined. 6. Gradually add this mixture to the Ninja Foodi PossibleCooker, stirring to incorporate. 7. Cover and switch the cooker to high for 15 to 20 minutes, allowing it to thicken while stirring occasionally.

Hearty Mixed Bean Soup

Prep time: 30 minutes | Cook time: 4 to 5 hours | Serves 6

- 3 (15-ounce / 425-g) cans pinto beans, undrained
- 3 (15-ounce / 425-g) cans Great Northern beans, undrained
- 4 cups chicken or vegetable broth
- 3 potatoes, peeled and chopped
- 4 carrots, sliced
- 2 celery ribs, sliced
- 1 large onion, chopped
- 1 green pepper, chopped
- 1 sweet red pepper, chopped (optional)
- 2 garlic cloves, minced
- 1 teaspoon salt, or to taste
- ¼ teaspoon pepper, or to taste
- 1 bay leaf (optional)
- ½ teaspoon liquid barbecue smoke (optional)

1. Empty beans into 6-quart Ninja Foodi PossibleCooker, or divide ingredients between 2 (4- to 5-quart) cookers. 2. Cover. Cook on low while preparing vegetables. 3. Cook broth and vegetables in stockpot until vegetables are tender-crisp. Transfer to Ninja Foodi PossibleCooker. 4. Add remaining ingredients and mix well. 5. Cover. Cook on low 4 to 5 hours. 6. Serve.

Pork and Vegetable Stew

Prep time: 15 minutes | Cook time: 6 hours | Serves 8

- 2 pounds (907 g) boneless pork loin, cut into 1-inch cubes
- 8 medium potatoes, peeled and cut into 2-inch pieces
- 6 large carrots, peeled and cut into 2-inch pieces
- 1 cup ketchup
- 2¼ cups water, divided

1. Brown pork cubes in a large nonstick skillet. 2. Lightly spray Ninja Foodi PossibleCooker with nonstick cooking spray. 3. Place all ingredients except ketchup and ¼ cup water in Ninja Foodi PossibleCooker. 4. Cover and cook on high 5 hours. One hour before serving, combine ketchup with ¼ cup water. Pour over stew. Cook one more hour.

Chili-Taco Stew

Prep time: 30 minutes | Cook time: 5 to 7 hours | Serves 8

- 2 pounds (907 g) lean stew meat
- 2 (15-ounce / 425-g) cans stewed tomatoes, Mexican or regular
- 1 envelope dry taco seasoning mix
- 2 (15-ounce / 425-g) cans pinto beans
- 1 (15-ounce / 425-g) can whole-kernel corn
- ¾ cup water

1. Cut large pieces of stew meat in half and brown in large nonstick skillet. 2. Combine all ingredients in Ninja Foodi PossibleCooker. 3. Cover and cook on low 5 to 7 hours.

Taco Chicken Soup

Prep time: 10 minutes | Cook time: 5 to 7 hours | Serves 4 to 6

- 1 envelope dry reduced-sodium taco seasoning
- 1 (32-ounce / 907-g) can low-sodium V-8 juice
- 1 (16-ounce / 454-g) jar salsa
- 1 (15-ounce / 425-g) can
- black beans
- 1 cup frozen corn
- 1 cup frozen peas
- 2 whole chicken breasts, cooked and shredded

1. In the Ninja Foodi PossibleCooker, mix all ingredients except for the corn, peas, and chicken. 2. Cover and cook on low for 4 to 6 hours. One hour before serving, add the corn, peas, and chicken to the cooker.

Potato Soup with Possibilities

Prep time: 20 minutes | Cook time: 5 to 6 hours | Serves 6

- 5 cups homemade chicken broth, or 2 (14-ounce / 397-g) cans chicken broth, plus ½ soup can water
- 1 large onion, chopped
- 3 celery stalks, chopped,
- including leaves, if you like
- 6 large white potatoes, peeled, chopped, cubed, or sliced
- Salt and pepper to taste

1. Add all ingredients to the Ninja Foodi PossibleCooker. 2. Cover and cook on high for 5 hours, or on low for 6 hours, until the vegetables are tender but not mushy.

Minestrone Soup

Prep time: 20 minutes | Cook time: 4 to 9 hours | Serves 8 to 10

- 1 large onion, chopped
- 4 carrots, sliced
- 3 ribs celery, sliced
- 2 garlic cloves, minced
- 1 tablespoon olive oil
- 1 (6-ounce / 170-g) can tomato paste
- 1 (14½-ounce / 411-g) can chicken, beef, or vegetable broth
- 1 (24-ounce / 680-g) can pinto beans, undrained
- 1 (10-ounce / 283-g) package
- frozen green beans
- 2 to 3 cups chopped cabbage
- 1 medium zucchini, sliced
- 8 cups water
- 2 tablespoons parsley
- 2 tablespoons Italian spice
- 1 teaspoon salt, or more
- ½ teaspoon pepper
- ¾ cup dry acini di pepe (small round pasta)
- Grated Parmesan or Asiago cheese

1. Sauté onion, carrots, celery, and garlic in oil until tender. 2. Combine all ingredients except pasta and cheese in Ninja Foodi PossibleCooker. 3. Cover. Cook 4 to 5 hours on high or 8 to 9 hours on low, adding pasta 1 hour before cooking is complete. 4. Top individual servings with cheese.

Zesty Mexican Rice and Bean Soup

Prep time: 15 minutes | Cook time: 6 hours | Serves 6

- ½ cup chopped onions
- ⅓ cup chopped green peppers
- 1 garlic clove, minced
- 1 tablespoon oil
- 1 (4-ounce / 113-g) package sliced or chipped dried beef
- 1 (18-ounce / 510-g) can tomato juice
- 1 (15½-ounce / 439-g) can red kidney beans, undrained
- 1½ cups water
- ½ cup long-grain rice, uncooked
- 1 teaspoon paprika
- ½ to 1 teaspoon chili powder
- ½ teaspoon salt
- Dash of pepper

1. Cook onions, green peppers, and garlic in oil in skillet until vegetables are tender but not brown. Transfer to Ninja Foodi PossibleCooker. 2. Tear beef into small pieces and add to Ninja Foodi PossibleCooker. 3. Add remaining ingredients. Mix well. 4. Cover. Cook on low 6 hours. Stir before serving. 5. Serve.

Bratwurst Stew

Prep time: 15 minutes | Cook time: 3 to 4 hours | Serves 8

- 2 (10¾-ounce / 305-g) cans fat-free chicken broth
- 4 medium carrots, sliced
- 2 ribs of celery, cut in chunks
- 1 medium onion, chopped
- 1 teaspoon dried basil
- ½ teaspoon garlic powder
- 3 cups chopped cabbage
- 2 (1-pound / 454-g) cans Great Northern beans, drained
- 5 fully cooked bratwurst links, cut into ½-inch slices

1. Add all ingredients to the Ninja Foodi PossibleCooker. 2. Set to cook on high for 3 to 4 hours, or until the vegetables are tender.

Sunday Chicken and Dumpling Stew

Prep time: 30 minutes | Cook time: 6½ hours | Serves 6

- ½ cup all-purpose flour
- 1 teaspoon salt
- ½ teaspoon white pepper
- 1 (3-pound / 1.4-kg) broiler/fryer chicken, cut up and skin removed
- 2 tablespoons canola oil
- 3 cups chicken broth

Dumplings:
- 1 cup all-purpose flour
- 2 teaspoons baking powder
- ½ teaspoon salt

- 6 large carrots, cut into 1-inch pieces
- 2 celery ribs, cut into ½-inch pieces
- 1 large sweet onion, thinly sliced
- 1 teaspoon dried rosemary, crushed
- 1½ cups frozen peas

- ½ teaspoon dried rosemary, crushed
- 1 egg, lightly beaten
- ½ cup 2% milk

1. In a large resealable plastic bag, combine the flour, salt and pepper; add chicken, a few pieces at a time, and shake to coat. In a large skillet, brown chicken in oil; remove and keep warm. Gradually add broth to the skillet; bring to a boil. 2. In a 5-quart Ninja Foodi PossibleCooker, layer carrots, celery and onion; sprinkle with rosemary. Add the chicken and hot broth. Cover and cook on low for 6 to 8 hours or until chicken and vegetables are tender and stew is bubbling. 3. Remove chicken; when cool enough to handle, remove meat from the bones and discard bones. Cut meat into bite-size pieces and return to the Ninja Foodi PossibleCooker. Stir in peas. 4. For dumplings, in a small bowl, combine the flour, baking powder, salt and rosemary. Combine the egg and milk; stir into dry ingredients. Drop by heaping teaspoonfuls onto simmering chicken mixture. Cover and cook on high for 25 to 30 minutes or until a toothpick inserted in a dumpling comes out clean (do not lift the cover while simmering).

Hearty Vegetarian Chili Soup

Prep time: 10 minutes | Cook time: 4 to 9½ hours | Serves 8

- 1 large onion, chopped
- 1 tablespoon margarine
- 1 clove garlic, finely chopped
- 2 teaspoons chili powder
- ½ teaspoon dried oregano, crumbled
- 2 (14½-ounce / 411-g) cans vegetable broth
- 1 (14½-ounce / 411-g) can
- no-salt-added stewed or diced tomatoes
- 5 cups water
- ½ teaspoon salt
- ¼ teaspoon black pepper
- ¾ pound (340 g) fresh kale
- ⅓ cup white long-grain rice
- 1 (19-ounce / 539-g) can cannellini beans, drained and rinsed

1. Sauté onion in skillet with margarine until tender. 2. Add garlic, chili powder, and oregano. Cook for 30 seconds. Pour into Ninja Foodi PossibleCooker. 3. Add remaining ingredients except kale, rice, and beans. 4. Cover. Cook on low 7 hours, or on high 3 to 4 hours. 5. Cut kale stalks into small pieces and chop leaves coarsely. 6. Add to soup with rice and beans. 7. Cover. Cook on high 1 to 2½ hours more, or until rice is tender and kale is done to your liking.

Chicken Stew with Gnocchi

Prep time: 15 minutes | Cook time: 8 hours | Serves 2

- 4 boneless, skinless chicken thighs, cubed
- 1 leek, white part only, chopped
- 2 garlic cloves, minced
- 1 sweet potato, peeled and chopped
- ½ cup chopped tomato
- ½ teaspoon salt
- ½ teaspoon dried basil leaves
- ⅛ teaspoon freshly ground black pepper
- 3 cups chicken stock
- 1 cup potato gnocchi

1. In the Ninja Foodi PossibleCooker, mix all ingredients except for the gnocchi. 2. Cover and cook on low for 7½ hours. 3. Add the gnocchi, cover again, and cook on high for an additional 25 to 30 minutes, or until the gnocchi are tender. 4. Serve the stew by ladling it into two bowls.

Savory Shrimp and Corn Delight

Prep time: 20 minutes | Cook time: 3 to 4 hours | Serves 6

- 3 slices lean turkey bacon, diced
- 1 cup chopped onions
- 2 cups diced, unpeeled red potatoes
- 2 (10-ounce / 283-g) packages frozen corn
- 1 teaspoon Worcestershire sauce
- ½ teaspoon paprika
- ½ teaspoon salt
- ¼ teaspoon black pepper
- 2 (6-ounce / 170-g) cans shrimp, drained
- 2 cups water
- 2 tablespoons butter
- 1 (12-ounce / 340-g) can fat-free evaporated milk
- Chopped chives

1. Brown bacon in nonstick skillet until lightly crisp. Add onions to drippings and sauté until transparent. Using slotted spoon, transfer bacon and onions to Ninja Foodi PossibleCooker. 2. Add remaining ingredients to cooker except milk and chives. 3. Cover. Cook on low 3 to 4 hours, adding milk and chives 30 minutes before end of cooking time.

Spiced-Pumpkin Chicken Soup

Prep time: 15 minutes | Cook time: 6 hours | Serves 6

- 1 tablespoon extra-virgin olive oil
- 4 cups chicken broth
- 2 cups coconut milk
- 1 pound (454 g) pumpkin, diced
- ½ sweet onion, chopped
- 1 tablespoon grated fresh ginger
- 2 teaspoons minced garlic
- ½ teaspoon ground cinnamon
- ¼ teaspoon ground nutmeg
- ¼ teaspoon freshly ground black pepper
- ¼ teaspoon salt
- Pinch ground allspice
- 1 cup heavy (whipping) cream
- 2 cups chopped cooked chicken

1. Lightly coat the insert of the Ninja Foodi PossibleCooker with olive oil. 2. In the insert, combine the broth, coconut milk, pumpkin, onion, ginger, garlic, cinnamon, nutmeg, pepper, salt, and allspice. 3. Cover and cook on low for 6 hours. 4. Use an immersion blender or a regular blender to purée the soup until smooth. 5. If you transferred the soup to a blender, return it to the pot and stir in the cream and chicken. 6. Continue heating the soup on low for 15 minutes to warm the chicken, then serve hot.

Karen's Hearty Split Pea Soup

Prep time: 15 minutes | Cook time: 7 hours | Serves 6

- 2 carrots
- 2 ribs celery
- 1 onion
- 1 parsnip
- 1 leek (keep 3 inches of green)
- 1 ripe tomato
- 1 ham hock
- 1¾ cups dried split peas, washed with stones removed
- 2 tablespoons olive oil
- 1 bay leaf
- 1 teaspoon dried thyme
- 4 cups chicken broth
- 4 cups water
- 1 teaspoon salt
- ¼ teaspoon pepper
- 2 teaspoons chopped fresh parsley

1. Cut all vegetables into ¼-inch pieces and place in Ninja Foodi PossibleCooker. Add remaining ingredients except salt, pepper, and parsley. 2. Cover. Cook on high 7 hours. 3. Remove ham hock. Shred meat from bone and return meat to pot. 4. Season soup with salt and pepper. Stir in parsley. Serve immediately

- Bean and Ham Soup
- Prep time: 30 minutes | Cook time: 9 to 11 hours | Serves 10
- 1 pound (454 g) mixed dry beans
- Ham bone from half a ham butt
- 1½ cups ham, cubed
- 1 large chopped onion
- ¾ cup chopped celery
- ¾ cup sliced or chopped carrots
- 1 (15-ounce / 425-g) can low-sodium diced tomatoes
- 2 tablespoons chopped parsley
- 1 cup low-sodium tomato juice
- 5 cups water
- 2 tablespoons Worcestershire sauce
- 1 bay leaf
- 1 teaspoon prepared mustard
- ½ teaspoon chili powder
- Juice of 1 lemon
- 1 teaspoon salt
- ½ teaspoon black pepper

1. Place the beans in a saucepan, cover with water, and soak overnight. Drain the beans the next day. 2. Add fresh water to the beans and cook them in the saucepan for 30 minutes uncovered. Drain again and discard the water. 3. In the Ninja Foodi PossibleCooker, combine the beans with all remaining ingredients. 4. Cover and cook on low for 9 to 11 hours. 5. Before serving, remove the bay leaf and ham bone.

Classic Chicken and Homemade Dumplings

Prep time: 30 minutes | Cook time: 4¼ to 6¼ hours | Serves 8

Soup:

- 4 cups cooked chicken, cubed
- 6 cups fat-free, low-sodium chicken broth
- 1 tablespoon fresh parsley, or 1½ teaspoons dry parsley flakes
- 1 cup onions, chopped
- 1 cup celery, chopped
- 6 cups diced potatoes
- 1 cup green beans
- 1 cup carrots
- 1 cup peas (optional)

Dumplings: (optional)

- 2 cups flour (half white and half whole wheat)
- 1 teaspoon salt
- 4 teaspoons baking powder
- 1 egg, beaten
- 2 tablespoons olive oil
- ⅔ cup skim milk

1. Combine all soup ingredients, except peas. 2. Cover. Cook on low 4 to 6 hours. 3. Transfer to large soup kettle with lid. Add peas, if desired. Bring to a boil. Reduce to simmer. 4. To make Dumplings, combine flour, salt, and baking powder in a large bowl. 5. In a separate bowl, combine egg, olive oil, and milk until smooth. Add to flour mixture.

Vegetable Salmon Chowder

Prep time: 15 minutes | Cook time: 3 hours | Serves 8

- 1½ cups cubed potatoes
- 1 cup diced celery
- ½ cup diced onions
- 2 tablespoons fresh parsley, or 1 tablespoon dried parsley
- ½ teaspoon salt
- ¼ teaspoon black pepper
- Water to cover
- 1 (16-ounce / 454-g) can pink salmon
- 4 cups skim milk
- 2 teaspoons lemon juice
- 2 tablespoons finely cut red bell peppers
- 2 tablespoons finely shredded carrots
- ½ cup instant potatoes

1. In the Ninja Foodi PossibleCooker, combine the cubed potatoes, celery, onions, parsley, salt, pepper, and enough water to cover the ingredients. 2. Cook on high for 3 hours, or until the vegetables are soft, adding more water if necessary. 3. Stir in the salmon, milk, lemon juice, red peppers, carrots, and instant potatoes. 4. Continue cooking for an additional hour until everything is very hot.

Spicy Lamb and Herb Soup

Prep time: 12 minutes | Cook time: 4 to 6 hours | Serves 6

- 1 pound (454 g) trimmed, boneless lamb neck or goat meat, cut into ¾-inch chunks
- 1 teaspoon salt
- 8½ cups hot water
- 1 teaspoon ghee
- 1 onion, sliced
- ½ teaspoon black pepper
- 2 fresh green chiles, chopped
- Handful fresh coriander leaves, chopped
- Handful fresh mint leaves, chopped
- Lime juice

1. Preheat the Ninja Foodi PossibleCooker on high. 2. Spray a little nonstick cooking spray inside and very quickly sear the meat. 3. Turn the cooker to low, and add the salt and the hot water. Cover and cook on low for 6 hours, or on high for 4 hours. 4. When the lamb is tender, heat the ghee in a frying pan and add the onions. Sauté them for about 5 minutes, until they brown. Add them to the Ninja Foodi PossibleCooker with the black pepper, green chiles, coriander leaves, mint, and a squeeze of lime. Mix into the soup and leave to heat through for 15 minutes. 5. Check the seasonings and serve.

South Indian Tomato and Pepper Soup

Prep time: 15 minutes | Cook time: 3 to 6 hours | Serves 6

- 6⅓ cups hot water
- ⅓ cup split yellow pigeon peas
- 1 tablespoon tamarind paste
- 1 heaped teaspoon black peppercorns
- 1 heaped teaspoon cumin seeds
- 1 teaspoon turmeric
- 20 curry leaves
- 6 tomatoes, roughly chopped
- 2 dried red chiles
- 4 garlic cloves, roughly chopped
- 4-inch piece fresh ginger, roughly chopped
- Handful coriander stalks, finely chopped
- Coriander leaves to garnish

1. Add all ingredients to the Ninja Foodi PossibleCooker. Cover and cook on low for 6 hours, or on high for 3 to 4 hours. 2. Use an immersion blender or a regular blender to create a smooth purée. 3. Taste the soup and adjust the salt if needed. 4. Serve garnished with coriander leaves.

Lamb Stew

Prep time: 35 minutes | Cook time: 8 to 10 hours | Serves 6

- 2 pounds (907 g) lean lamb, cubed
- ½ teaspoon sugar
- 2 tablespoons canola oil
- 1½ teaspoons salt
- ¼ teaspoon black pepper
- ¼ cup flour
- 2 cups water
- ¾ cup red cooking wine
- ¼ teaspoon garlic powder
- 2 teaspoons Worcestershire sauce
- 6 to 8 carrots, sliced
- 4 small onions, quartered
- 4 ribs celery, sliced
- 3 medium potatoes, diced

1. Sprinkle lamb with sugar. Brown in oil in skillet. 2. Remove lamb and place in cooker, reserving drippings. Stir salt, pepper, and flour into drippings in skillet until smooth. Stir in water and wine until smooth, stirring loose the meat drippings. Continue cooking and stirring occasionally until broth simmers and thickens. 3. Pour into cooker. Add remaining ingredients and stir until well mixed. 4. Cover. Cook on low 8 to 10 hours.

Lemon Garlic Chicken and Kale Soup

Prep time: 15 minutes | Cook time: 6 hours | Serves 2

- 2 boneless, skinless chicken thighs, diced
- 1 small onion, halved and sliced thin
- 2 carrots, peeled and diced
- 6 garlic cloves, roughly chopped
- 2 cups low-sodium chicken broth
- ⅛ teaspoon sea salt
- ⅛ teaspoon red pepper flakes
- Zest of 1 lemon
- Juice of 1 lemon
- 2 cups shredded fresh kale

1. Put the chicken, onion, carrots, garlic, broth, salt, red pepper flakes, and lemon zest in the Ninja Foodi PossibleCooker and stir to combine. 2. Cover and cook on low for 6 hours. 3. Stir in the lemon juice and kale just before serving.

Rich and Creamy Potato Corn Chowder

Prep time: 30 minutes | Cook time: 2 hours | Serves 12

- ½ pound (227 g) lean turkey bacon
- 4 cups diced potatoes
- 2 cups chopped onions
- 2 cups fat-free sour cream
- 1½ cups fat-free milk
- 2 (10¾-ounce / 305-g) cans fat-free, low-sodium cream of chicken soup
- 2 (15¼-ounce / 432-g) cans fat-free, low-sodium whole-kernel corn, undrained

1. Cut bacon into 1-inch pieces. Cook for 5 minutes in large nonstick skillet, doing it in two batches so all the pieces brown. 2. Add potatoes and onions and a bit of water. Cook 15 to 20 minutes, until vegetables are tender, stirring occasionally. Drain. Transfer to Ninja Foodi PossibleCooker. 3. Combine sour cream, milk, chicken soup, and corn. Place in Ninja Foodi PossibleCooker. 4. Cover. Cook on low for 2 hours.

Hamburger Vegetable Stew

Prep time: 20 minutes | Cook time: 8 to 10 hours | Serves 8

- 2 pounds (907 g) ground beef
- 1 medium onion, chopped
- 1 garlic clove, minced
- 2 cups tomato juice
- 2 to 3 carrots, sliced
- 2 to 3 ribs celery, sliced
- Half a green pepper, chopped
- 2 cups green beans
- 2 medium potatoes, cubed
- 2 cups water
- 1 tablespoon Worcestershire sauce
- ¼ teaspoon dried oregano
- ¼ teaspoon dried basil
- ¼ teaspoon dried thyme
- Dash of hot pepper sauce
- 2 tablespoons dry onion soup mix, or 1 beef bouillon cube
- 1 teaspoon salt
- ¼ teaspoon pepper

1. In a saucepan, brown the meat and onion, then drain any excess fat. Stir in the garlic and tomato juice, and bring to a boil. 2. Transfer all ingredients to the Ninja Foodi PossibleCooker. 3. Cover and cook on low for 8 to 10 hours.

Toscano Soup

Prep time: 20 minutes | Cook time: 6 to 8 hours | Serves 4 to 6

- 2 medium russet potatoes
- 1 pound (454 g) spicy Italian sausage
- 5½ cups chicken stock or low-sodium chicken broth
- 2 cups chopped kale
- ½ teaspoon crushed red pepper flakes (optional)
- ½ cup cream or evaporated milk

1. Dice the potatoes into ½-inch cubes and place them in the Ninja Foodi PossibleCooker. 2. Grill, broil, or brown the sausage in a nonstick skillet. Once it's cool enough to handle, slice it into ½-inch thick rounds. 3. Add the sliced sausage to the Ninja Foodi PossibleCooker, then stir in all remaining ingredients except for the cream. 4. Cover and cook on low for 6 to 8 hours. 5. About 15 to 20 minutes before serving, add the cream or evaporated milk and cook until the soup is heated through.

Tortilla Soup

Prep time: 10 minutes | Cook time: 3 to 4 hours | Serves 7

- 1 (16-ounce / 454-g) can fat-free refried beans
- 1 (15-ounce / 425-g) can black beans, rinsed and drained
- 1 (14-ounce / 397-g) fat-free chicken broth
- 1½ cups frozen corn
- ¾ cup chunky salsa
- ¾ cup boneless, skinless cooked chicken, cubed
- ¼ cup water
- 2 cups reduced-fat shredded cheese, divided
- 1 bag baked tortilla chips

1. Mix all ingredients in the Ninja Foodi PossibleCooker, except for the cheese and chips. 2. Cook on low for 3 to 4 hours, or until the mixture is heated through. 3. Stir in half of the cheese and mix until melted. 4. Crush the chips in bowls, then ladle the soup over them. Top with sour cream and additional crushed chips.

Ham and Potato Chowder

Prep time: 10 minutes | Cook time: 8 hours | Serves 5

- 1 (5-ounce / 142-g) package scalloped potatoes
- Sauce mix from potato package
- 1 cup cooked ham, cut into narrow strips
- 4 cups chicken broth
- 1 cup chopped celery
- ⅓ cup chopped onions
- Salt to taste
- Pepper to taste
- 2 cups half-and-half
- ⅓ cup flour

1. In the Ninja Foodi PossibleCooker, mix together the potatoes, sauce mix, ham, broth, celery, onions, salt, and pepper. 2. Cover and cook on low for 7 hours. 3. In a bowl, combine the half-and-half with flour until smooth. Gradually add this mixture to the Ninja Foodi PossibleCooker, blending thoroughly. 4. Cover and continue cooking on low for up to 1 hour, stirring occasionally until the mixture has thickened.

Hearty Sausage and Vegetable Medley

Prep time: 30 minutes | Cook time: 3 to 10 hours | Serves 10

- 1 pound (454 g) sausage (regular, turkey, or smoked)
- 4 cups potatoes, cooked and cubed
- 4 cups carrots, cooked and sliced
- 4 cups green beans, cooked
- 1 (28-ounce / 794-g) can tomato sauce
- 1 teaspoon onion powder
- ¼ or ½ teaspoon black pepper, according to your taste

1. Slice sausage into 1½-inch pieces. Place in Ninja Foodi PossibleCooker. 2. Add cooked vegetables. Pour tomato sauce over top. 3. Sprinkle with onion powder and pepper. Stir. 4. Cook on high 3 to 4 hours, or on low 8 to 10 hours.

Green Bean and Ham Soup

Prep time: 15 minutes | Cook time: 4¼ to 6¼ hours | Serves 6

- 1 meaty ham bone, or 2 cups cubed ham
- 1½ quarts water
- 1 large onion, chopped
- 2 to 3 cups cut-up green beans
- 3 large carrots, sliced
- 2 large potatoes, peeled and cubed

- 1 tablespoon parsley
- 1 tablespoon summer savory
- ½ teaspoon salt
- ¼ teaspoon pepper
- 1 cup cream or milk

1. In the Ninja Foodi PossibleCooker, mix all ingredients except for the cream. 2. Cover and cook on high for 4 to 6 hours. 3. Remove the ham bone, cut the meat off, and return the meat to the Ninja Foodi PossibleCooker. 4. Switch to low, stir in the cream or milk, and heat through before serving.

Hungarian Barley Stew

Prep time: 20 minutes | Cook time: 5 hours | Serves 8

- 2 tablespoons oil
- 1½ pounds (680 g) beef cubes
- 2 large onions, diced
- 1 medium green pepper, chopped
- 1 (28-ounce / 794-g) can whole tomatoes
- ½ cup ketchup
- ⅔ cup dry small pearl barley

- 1 teaspoon salt
- ½ teaspoon pepper
- 1 tablespoon paprika
- 1 (10-ounce / 283-g) package frozen baby lima beans
- 3 cups water
- 1 cup sour cream

1. In a skillet, brown the beef cubes in oil, then add the onions and green peppers and sauté until softened. Transfer this mixture to the Ninja Foodi PossibleCooker. 2. Add all remaining ingredients except for the sour cream. 3. Cover the Ninja Foodi PossibleCooker and cook on high for 5 hours. 4. Before serving, stir in the sour cream. 5. Serve hot.

Zesty Taco Pasta Soup

Prep time: 10 minutes | Cook time: 4 to 6 hours | Serves 6 to 8

- 1 medium onion, chopped
- 2 garlic cloves, minced
- 2 tablespoons canola or olive oil
- 3 cups reduced-sodium beef broth or vegetable broth
- 1 (15-ounce / 425-g) can black beans, rinsed and drained
- 1 (14½-ounce / 411-g) can diced tomatoes, undrained
- 1½ cups picante sauce

- 1 cup spiral pasta, uncooked
- 1 small green bell pepper, chopped
- 2 teaspoons chili powder
- 1 teaspoon ground cumin
- ½ cup shredded reduced-fat cheese
- Fat-free sour cream (optional)

1. Sauté onions and garlic in oil in skillet. 2. Combine all ingredients except cheese and sour cream. 3. Cook on low 4 to 6 hours, or just until pasta is tender. 4. Add cheese and sour cream as desired when serving.

Chapter
7

Snacks and Appetizers

Chapter 7 Snacks and Appetizers

Tangy Barbecue Meatball Bites

Prep time: 30 minutes | Cook time: 2¼ hours | Serves 16

- 1 pound (454 g) ground beef
- ¼ cup finely chopped onion
- 1 (16-ounce / 454-g) package miniature hot dogs, drained
- 1 (12-ounce / 340-g) jar apricot preserves
- 1 cup barbecue sauce
- 1 (20-ounce / 567-g) can pineapple chunks, drained

1. In a large bowl, combine beef and onion, mixing lightly but thoroughly. Shape into 1-inch balls. In a large skillet over medium heat, cook meatballs in two batches until cooked through, turning occasionally. 2. Using a slotted spoon, transfer meatballs to a 3-quart Ninja Foodi PossibleCooker. Add the hot dogs; stir in the preserves and barbecue sauce. Cook, covered, on high 2 to 3 hours or until heated through. 3. Stir in the pineapple; cook, covered, 15 to 20 minutes longer or until mixture is heated through.

Refried Bean Dip

Prep time: 20 minutes | Cook time: 2 to 3 hours | Serves 8

- 8 ounces (227 g) spicy sausages, such as chorizo, andouille, or Italian, removed from its casing
- 1 medium onion, chopped
- 2 Anaheim chiles, seeded and chopped
- 1 medium red or yellow bell pepper, seeded and chopped
- 2 (14- to 15-ounce / 397- to
- 425-g) cans refried beans (nonfat are fine here)
- 2 cups finely shredded mild Cheddar cheese, or 1 cup each finely shredded Monterey Jack and sharp Cheddar cheese
- 2 tablespoons finely chopped fresh cilantro
- Tortilla chips for serving

1. Lightly coat the insert of a 1½- to 3-quart Ninja Foodi PossibleCooker with nonstick cooking spray. In a medium skillet over high heat, cook the sausage until it's no longer pink, breaking up large pieces with a spoon. Drain the sausage and transfer it to a mixing bowl to cool. In the same skillet, sauté the onion, chiles, and bell pepper until the bell pepper is softened, about 5 minutes. Add this mixture to the bowl with the sausage and let it cool slightly. Then, stir in the refried beans until well combined. 2. Layer half of the bean mixture in the Ninja Foodi PossibleCooker and sprinkle with half of the cheese. Add the remaining bean mixture on top, followed by the rest of the cheese and a sprinkle of cilantro. Cover and cook on low for 2 to 3 hours. 3. Serve directly from the cooker, keeping it on warm, and enjoy with sturdy tortilla chips.

Cheesy Loaded Vegetable Delight

Prep time: 1 hour | Cook time: 1 hour | Makes 5 cups

- ¾ cup finely chopped fresh broccoli
- ½ cup finely chopped cauliflower
- ½ cup finely chopped fresh carrot
- ½ cup finely chopped red onion
- ½ cup finely chopped celery
- 2 garlic cloves, minced
- 4 tablespoons olive oil, divided
- 1 (14-ounce / 397-g) can water-packed artichoke hearts, rinsed, drained and chopped
- 1 (6½-ounce / 184-g)
- package spreadable garlic and herb cream cheese
- 1 (1.4-ounce / 40-g) package vegetable recipe mix (Knorr)
- 1 teaspoon garlic powder
- ½ teaspoon white pepper
- ⅛ to ¼ teaspoon cayenne pepper
- ¼ cup vegetable broth
- ¼ cup half-and-half cream
- 3 cups shredded Italian cheese blend
- ½ cup minced fresh basil
- 1 (9-ounce / 255-g) package fresh spinach, finely chopped
- Assorted crackers or baked pita chips

1. In a large skillet, saute the broccoli, cauliflower, carrot, onion, celery and garlic in 2 tablespoons oil until tender. Stir in the artichokes, cream cheese, vegetable recipe mix, garlic powder, white pepper and cayenne; set aside. 2. In a 3-quart Ninja Foodi PossibleCooker, combine broth, cream and remaining oil. Stir in broccoli mixture, Italian cheese blend and basil. Fold in spinach. Cover and cook on low for 1 to 2 hours or until cheese is melted and spinach is tender. Serve with crackers.

The Best Artichoke Spinach Dip on the Planet

Prep time: 15 minutes | Cook time: 2 to 3 hours | Serves 8

- 6 strips bacon, cut into ½-inch pieces
- 1 medium onion, finely chopped
- 1 (16-ounce / 454-g) package frozen chopped spinach, defrosted and drained thoroughly
- 1 (16-ounce / 454-g) package frozen artichoke hearts, defrosted, drained,
- and coarsely chopped, or 2 (14- to 15-ounce / 397- to 425-g) cans artichoke hearts, drained and coarsely chopped
- ¼ teaspoon freshly ground black pepper
- 1½ cups mayonnaise
- 2 cups shredded sharp white Cheddar cheese

1. In a large skillet, cook the bacon until crispy, then transfer it to paper towels to drain. Leave about 2 tablespoons of the bacon drippings in the pan and heat it over medium-high heat. 2. Add the onion and sauté for about 2 minutes until it starts to soften. Then, add the spinach and artichoke hearts, cooking until the liquid in the pan has evaporated. Season with pepper, then transfer the mixture to the insert of a 1½- to 3-quart Ninja Foodi PossibleCooker. Stir in the mayonnaise and cheese until well combined. Cover and cook on low for 2 to 3 hours. 3. Before serving, garnish the dip with the bacon bits and keep it warm in the cooker.

Chocolate Peanut Cluster Treats

Prep time: 20 minutes | Cook time: 3 hours | Makes 3½ to 4 dozen pieces

- 2 pounds (907 g) white candy coating, chopped
- 1 (12-ounce / 340-g) package semi-sweet chocolate chips
- 1 (4-ounce / 113-g) milk chocolate bar, or 1 (4-ounce
- / 113-g) package German sweet chocolate, chopped
- 1 (24-ounce / 680-g) jar dry roasted peanuts
- Nonstick cooking spray

1. Spray inside of Ninja Foodi PossibleCooker with nonstick cooking spray. 2. In Ninja Foodi PossibleCooker, combine white candy coating, chocolate chips, and milk chocolate. 3. Cover and cook on low 3 hours. Stir every 15 minutes. 4. Add peanuts to melted chocolate. Mix well. 5. Drop by tablespoonfuls onto waxed paper. Cool until set. Serve immediately, or store in a tightly covered container, separating layers with waxed paper. Keep cool and dry.

Tangy Grape Jelly Meatball Bites

Prep time: 10 minutes | Cook time: 2 to 4 hours | Serves 15 to 20

- 1 (12-ounce / 340-g) jar grape jelly
- 1 (12-ounce / 340-g) jar chili sauce
- 2 (1-pound / 454-g) bags prepared frozen meatballs, thawed

1. Combine jelly and sauce in Ninja Foodi PossibleCooker. Stir well. 2. Add meatballs. Stir to coat. 3. Cover and heat on low 4 hours, or on high 2 hours. Keep Ninja Foodi PossibleCooker on low while serving.

Slim Dunk

Prep time: 10 minutes | Cook time: 1 hour | Serves 12

- 2 cups fat-free sour cream
- ¼ cup fat-free miracle whip salad dressing
- 1 (10-ounce / 283-g) package frozen chopped spinach,
- squeezed dry and chopped
- 1 (1.8-ounce / 51-g) envelope dry leek soup mix
- ¼ cup red bell pepper, minced

1. In the Ninja Foodi PossibleCooker, add all ingredients and mix thoroughly. 2. Cover and cook on high for 1 hour. 3. Serve warm.

Spicy Buffalo Chicken Dip

Prep time: 20 minutes | Cook time: 2 hours | Makes 6 cups

- 2 (8-ounce / 227-g) packages cream cheese, softened
- ½ cup ranch salad dressing
- ½ cup sour cream
- 5 tablespoons crumbled blue cheese
- 2 cups shredded cooked
- chicken
- ½ cup Buffalo wing sauce
- 2 cups shredded cheddar cheese, divided
- 1 green onion, sliced
- Tortilla chips

1. In a small bowl, combine the cream cheese, dressing, sour cream and blue cheese. Transfer to a 3-quart Ninja Foodi PossibleCooker. Layer with chicken, wing sauce and 1 cup cheese. Cover and cook on low for 2 to 3 hours or until heated through. 2. Sprinkle with remaining cheese and onion. Serve with tortilla chips.

Spicy Crocked Nuts

Prep time: 15 minutes | Cook time: 2 to 2½ hours | Serves 8

- 4 tablespoons (½ stick) unsalted butter, melted
- 2 teaspoons Lawry's seasoned salt
- 1 teaspoon garlic salt
- ⅛ teaspoon cayenne pepper
- 4 tablespoons sugar
- 4 cups pecan halves, walnut halves, or whole almonds

1. In the insert of a 5- to 7-quart Ninja Foodi PossibleCooker, combine the butter, seasoned salt, garlic salt, cayenne, and 2 tablespoons of sugar. Cover and cook on high for 20 minutes. 2. Add the nuts to the cooker and stir to coat them in the butter mixture. Cook uncovered for 2 to 2½ hours, stirring occasionally. 3. Once cooked, sprinkle the remaining 2 tablespoons of sugar over the nuts, toss to coat, and transfer them to a baking sheet to cool completely before serving.

Sweet and Spicy Smoked Sausage Bites

Prep time: 15 minutes | Cook time: 4 hours | Serves 16 to 20

- 2 (16-ounce / 454-g) packages miniature smoked sausage links
- 1 cup brown sugar, packed
- ½ cup ketchup
- ¼ cup prepared horseradish

1. Place sausages in Ninja Foodi PossibleCooker. 2. Combine remaining ingredients in a bowl and pour over sausages. 3. Cover and cook on low for 4 hours.

Sweet and Spicy Peanuts

Prep time: 10 minutes | Cook time: 1½ hours | Makes 4 cups

- 3 cups salted peanuts
- ½ cup sugar
- ⅓ cup packed brown sugar
- 2 tablespoons hot water
- 2 tablespoons butter, melted
- 1 tablespoon Sriracha Asian hot chili sauce or hot pepper sauce
- 1 teaspoon chili powder

1. Place the peanuts in a greased 1½-quart Ninja Foodi PossibleCooker. In a small bowl, mix together the sugars, water, butter, hot sauce, and chili powder. Pour this mixture over the peanuts. Cover and cook on high for 1½ hours, stirring once during cooking. 2. Once done, spread the peanuts on waxed paper to cool completely. Store them in an airtight container.

Warm Crab Dip

Prep time: 20 minutes | Cook time: 1½ hours | Makes 2⅓ cups

- 1 (8-ounce / 227-g) package cream cheese, softened
- 2 green onions, chopped
- ¼ cup chopped sweet red pepper
- 2 tablespoons minced fresh parsley
- 2 tablespoons mayonnaise
- 1 tablespoon Dijon mustard
- 1 teaspoon Worcestershire sauce
- ¼ teaspoon salt
- ¼ teaspoon pepper
- 2 (6-ounce / 170-g) cans lump crabmeat, drained
- 2 tablespoons capers, drained
- Dash hot pepper sauce
- Assorted crackers

1. In a 1½-quart Ninja Foodi PossibleCooker, mix the first nine ingredients, then gently fold in the crab. 2. Cover and cook on low for 1 to 2 hours. Stir in the capers and pepper sauce, and cook for an additional 30 minutes to let the flavors meld. Serve with crackers.

Sweet and Smoky BBQ Bites

Prep time: 5 minutes | Cook time: 4 hours | Serves 48 to 60 as an appetizer

- 4 (16-ounce / 454-g) packages little smokies
- 1 (18-ounce / 510-g) bottle barbecue sauce

1. Mix ingredients together in Ninja Foodi PossibleCooker. 2. Cover and cook on low for 4 hours.

Smokies

Prep time: 5 minutes | Cook time: 6 to 7 hours | Serves 12 to 16

- 2 pounds (907 g) miniature smoked sausage links
- 1 (28-ounce / 794-g) bottle barbecue sauce
- 1¼ cups water
- 3 tablespoons Worcestershire sauce
- 3 tablespoons steak sauce
- ½ teaspoon pepper

1. In the Ninja Foodi PossibleCooker, mix all ingredients together until well combined. 2. Cover and cook on low for 6 to 7 hours.

Savory Chex Snack Mix

Prep time: 10 minutes | Cook time: 2 hours | Serves 10 to 14

- 8 cups Chex cereal, of any combination
- 6 cups pretzels
- 6 tablespoons butter, melted
- 2 tablespoons Worcestershire
- sauce
- 1 teaspoon seasoned salt
- ½ teaspoon garlic powder
- ½ teaspoon onion salt
- ½ teaspoon onion powder

1. Combine first two ingredients in Ninja Foodi PossibleCooker. 2. Combine butter and seasonings. Pour over dry mixture. Toss until well mixed. 3. Cover. Cook on low 2 hours, stirring every 30 minutes.

Mini Hot Dogs

Prep time: 5 minutes | Cook time: 4 to 5 hours | Serves 20 to 30 as an appetizer

- 2 cups brown sugar
- 1 tablespoon Worcestershire sauce
- 1 (14-ounce / 397-g) bottle ketchup
- 2 or 3 pounds (907 g or 1.4 kg) mini-hot dogs

1. In the Ninja Foodi PossibleCooker, combine the brown sugar, Worcestershire sauce, and ketchup. Stir in the hot dogs until well coated. 2. Cover and cook on high for 1 hour, then reduce the heat to low and cook for an additional 3 to 4 hours. 3. Serve directly from the cooker while it's still on low.

Creamy Warm Clam Dip

Prep time: 15 minutes | Cook time: 2 to 3 hours | Serves 6 to 8

- 2 (8-ounce / 227-g) packages cream cheese at room temperature and cut into cubes
- ½ cup mayonnaise
- 3 green onions, finely chopped, using the white and tender green parts
- 2 cloves garlic, minced
- 3 (8-ounce / 227-g) cans minced or chopped clams, drained with ¼ cup clam juice reserved
- 1 tablespoon Worcestershire sauce
- 2 teaspoons anchovy paste
- ¼ cup finely chopped fresh Italian parsley

1. Coat the insert of a 1½- to 3-quart Ninja Foodi PossibleCooker with nonstick cooking spray. Combine all the ingredients in a large mixing bowl, adding the clam juice to thin the dip. 2. Transfer the mixture to the Ninja Foodi PossibleCooker, cover, and cook on low for 2 to 3 hours, until bubbling. 3. Serve from the cooker set on warm.

Southwestern Chili con Queso

Prep time: 20 minutes | Cook time: 2 to 3 hours | Serves 8

- 1 (8-ounce / 227-g) package cream cheese, cut into cubes
- 2 tablespoons unsalted butter
- 1 medium sweet onion, such as Vidalia, finely chopped
- 4 chipotle chiles in adobo, minced
- 1 medium red bell pepper, seeded and finely chopped
- 1 medium yellow bell
- pepper, seeded and finely chopped
- 2 teaspoons ground cumin
- 2 cups finely shredded sharp Cheddar cheese
- 2 cups finely shredded Monterey Jack cheese
- Fresh vegetables for serving
- Tortilla chips for serving

1. Spray the insert of a 1½- to 3-quart Ninja Foodi PossibleCooker with nonstick cooking spray. Turn the cooker to low and add the cream cheese. Cover and let it soften while you prepare the other ingredients. 2. In a large sauté pan, melt the butter over medium-high heat. Add the onion, chipotles, bell peppers, and cumin, sautéing for 4 to 5 minutes until the bell peppers are softened. Transfer this mixture to the Ninja Foodi PossibleCooker and stir to combine with the cream cheese. 3. Gently fold in the Cheddar and Jack cheeses. Cover and cook on low for 2 to 3 hours. 4. Serve warm from the cooker alongside fresh vegetables and sturdy tortilla chips.

Apple Kielbasa

Prep time: 15 minutes | Cook time: 6 to 8 hours | Serves 12

- 2 pounds (907 g) fully cooked kielbasa sausage, cut into 1-inch pieces
- ¾ cup brown sugar
- 1 cup chunky applesauce
- 2 cloves garlic, minced

1. In the Ninja Foodi PossibleCooker, mix all ingredients together. 2. Cover and cook on low for 6 to 8 hours, or until everything is thoroughly heated.

Spicy Orange Chipotle Chicken Wings

Prep time: 15 minutes | Cook time: 3 hours | Serves 8

- 3 pounds (1.4 kg) chicken wing drumettes
- 1 medium red onion, finely chopped
- 6 chipotle chiles in adobo, finely chopped
- 1 teaspoon ground cumin
- 2 cloves garlic, minced
- 1½ cups orange juice
- ½ cup honey
- ½ cup ketchup
- ½ cup finely chopped fresh cilantro

1. Coat the insert of a 5- to 7-quart Ninja Foodi PossibleCooker with nonstick cooking spray. 2. Arrange the wings on a rack in a baking sheet and broil until the wings are crispy on one side. 3. Turn the wings and broil until crispy and browned, another 5 minutes. 4. Remove the wings from the oven. If you would like to do this step ahead of time, cool the wings and refrigerate for up to 2 days; other wise, place the wings in the prepared slow-cooker insert. 5. Combine the remaining ingredients in a mixing bowl, pour over the wings, and turn the wings to coat with the sauce. 6. Cover and cook the wings on high for 3 hours, until they are cooked through; turn them twice during the cooking process to ensure even cooking. 7. Serve the wings from the cooker set on warm.

Crispy Snack Mix

Prep time: 10 minutes | Cook time: 2½ hours | Makes about 2½ quarts

- 4½ cups crispy chow mein noodles
- 4 cups Rice Chex
- 1 (9¾-ounce / 276-g) can salted cashews
- 1 cup flaked coconut, toasted
- ½ cup butter, melted
- 2 tablespoons reduced-sodium soy sauce
- 2¼ teaspoons curry powder
- ¾ teaspoon ground ginger

1. In a 5-quart Ninja Foodi PossibleCooker, mix together the noodles, cereal, cashews, and shredded coconut. In a separate bowl, whisk together melted butter, soy sauce, curry powder, and ginger until well combined. Drizzle this mixture over the dry ingredients and stir until everything is evenly coated. 2. Cover the Ninja Foodi PossibleCooker and set it to low heat for 2½ hours, stirring the mixture every 30 minutes to ensure even cooking. Once done, serve the dish warm or let it cool to room temperature before enjoying.

Tangy Pickled Whiting Fillets

Prep time: 10 minutes | Cook time: 3 to 4 hours | Serves 24

- 2 onions, sliced
- 1 cup white vinegar
- ¾ cup Splenda
- 1 teaspoon salt
- 1 tablespoon allspice
- 2 pounds (907 g) frozen individual whiting with skin

1. Combine onions, vinegar, Splenda, salt, and allspice in bottom of Ninja Foodi PossibleCooker. 2. Slice frozen whiting into 2-inch slices, each with skin on. Place fish in Ninja Foodi PossibleCooker, pushing it down into the liquid as much as possible. 3. Cook on low 3 to 4 hours. 4. Pour cooking liquid over fish, cover, and refrigerate. Serve when well chilled.

Reuben Spread

Prep time: 10 minutes | Cook time: 4 hours | Serves 3

- 2 (8-ounce / 227-g) packages cream cheese, cubed
- 4 cups shredded Swiss cheese
- 1 (14-ounce / 397-g) can sauerkraut, rinsed and well drained
- 4 (2-ounce / 57-g) packages thinly sliced deli corned beef, chopped
- ½ cup Thousand Island salad dressing
- Snack rye bread or rye crackers

1. In a 1½-quart Ninja Foodi PossibleCooker, combine the first five ingredients and mix well. Cover and cook on low for 4 to 4½ hours, or until everything is heated through. 2. Once cooked, stir to combine and serve warm, spread on your favorite bread.

Cheesy Green Chili Casserole

Prep time: 15 minutes | Cook time: 6 to 8 hours | Serves 8

- 1¼ cups milk
- 4 eggs, beaten
- 3 tablespoons flour
- 1 (12-ounce / 340-g) can chopped green chilies
- 2 cups shredded Cheddar cheese

1. Combine all ingredients in Ninja Foodi PossibleCooker until well blended. 2. Cover and cook on low for 6 to 8 hours. 3. Serve.

Rich Cranberry-Glazed Meatballs

Prep time: 15 minutes | Cook time: 2 to 6 hours | Serves 6

- 50 meatballs, about 1½ pounds (680 g)
- 1 cup brown gravy, from a jar, or made from a mix
- 1 cup whole-berry cranberry sauce
- 2 tablespoons heavy cream
- 2 teaspoons Dijon mustard

1. Put meatballs in Ninja Foodi PossibleCooker. 2. Mix remaining ingredients in a bowl. Pour over meatballs. 3. Cover and cook on high 2 to 3 hours or on low 5 to 6 hours.

Hot Dill and Swiss Dip

Prep time: 10 minutes | Cook time: 2 to 3 hours | Serves 8

- 2 medium sweet onions, such as Vidalia, finely chopped
- 2 tablespoons finely chopped fresh dill
- 1½ cups mayonnaise
- 2 cups finely shredded Havarti with dill
- 2 cups finely shredded Swiss cheese

1. Lightly grease the insert of a 1½- to 3-quart Ninja Foodi PossibleCooker with nonstick cooking spray. In a separate bowl, mix all the ingredients together, then transfer the mixture to the Ninja Foodi PossibleCooker. Cover and cook on low for 2 to 3 hours, or until the mixture is bubbling. 2. Keep the cooker set on warm while serving directly from it.

Ultimate All-American Snack Mix

Prep time: 10 minutes | Cook time: 3 hours | Makes 3 quarts snack mix

- 3 cups thin pretzel sticks
- 4 cups Wheat Chex
- 4 cups Cheerios
- 1 (12-ounce / 340-g) can salted peanuts
- ¼ cup butter, melted
- 1 teaspoon garlic powder
- 1 teaspoon celery salt
- ½ teaspoon seasoned salt
- 2 tablespoons grated Parmesan cheese

1. Combine pretzels, cereal, and peanuts in large bowl. 2. Melt butter. Stir in garlic powder, celery salt, seasoned salt, and Parmesan cheese. Pour over pretzels and cereal. Toss until well mixed. 3. Pour into large Ninja Foodi PossibleCooker. Cover. Cook on low 2½ hours, stirring every 30 minutes. Remove lid and cook another 30 minutes on low. 4. Serve warm or at room temperature. Store in tightly covered container.

Chili Nuts

Prep time: 5 minutes | Cook time: 2 to 2½ hours | Makes 5 cups nuts

- ¼ cup butter, melted
- 2 (12-ounce / 340-g) cans cocktail peanuts
- 1 (1.6-ounce / 45-g) package chili seasoning mix

1. In the Ninja Foodi PossibleCooker, drizzle the melted butter over the nuts. 2. Add the dry chili mix and toss everything together until the nuts are well coated. Cover and cook on low for 2 to 2½ hours. Then, turn the heat to high, remove the lid, and cook for an additional 10 to 15 minutes. 3. Serve warm or let cool before enjoying.

Savory Curried Almonds

Prep time: 5 minutes | Cook time: 3 to 4½ hours | Makes 4 cups nuts

- 2 tablespoons butter, melted
- 1 tablespoon curry powder
- ½ teaspoon seasoned salt
- 1 pound (454 g) blanched almonds

1. Combine butter with curry powder and seasoned salt. 2. Pour over almonds in Ninja Foodi PossibleCooker. Mix to coat well. 3. Cover. Cook on low 2 to 3 hours. Turn to high. Uncover cooker and cook 1 to 1½ hours. 4. Serve hot or cold.

Meaty Buffet Favorites

Prep time: 5 minutes | Cook time: 2 hours | Serves 24

- 1 cup tomato sauce
- 1 teaspoon Worcestershire sauce
- ½ teaspoon prepared mustard
- 2 tablespoons brown sugar
- 1 pound (454 g) prepared meatballs or mini-wieners

1. In the Ninja Foodi PossibleCooker, combine the first four ingredients and mix well. 2. Add the meatballs or mini-wieners, stirring to coat them in the mixture. 3. Cover and cook on high for 2 hours. After that, switch to low and serve as an appetizer directly from the Ninja Foodi PossibleCooker.

Chapter

8

Vegetables and Sides

Chapter 8 Vegetables and Sides

Stuffed Peppers with Beans

Prep time: 15 minutes | Cook time: 6 hours | Serves 4

- 4 medium green, yellow, or red sweet peppers, or a mixture of colors
- 1 cup rice, cooked
- 1 (15-ounce / 425-g) can chili beans with chili gravy
- 1 cup shredded cheese, divided
- 1 (14½-ounce / 411-g) can petite diced tomatoes, with onion, celery, and green pepper

1. Rinse and dry the sweet peppers, then cut off the tops and remove the membranes and seeds, ensuring the peppers remain whole. 2. In a mixing bowl, combine the rice, beans, and half of the cheese, then spoon this mixture into the prepared peppers. 3. Pour the tomatoes into the Ninja Foodi PossibleCooker and arrange the stuffed peppers on top, keeping them upright and not stacking them. 4. Cover and cook on high for 3 hours. 5. Once cooked, carefully remove the peppers from the cooker and place them on a serving platter. Drizzle the hot tomatoes over the peppers and sprinkle the remaining cheese on top.

Spinach and Paneer Cheese

Prep time: 15 minutes | Cook time: 2 to 4 hours | Serves 6

- 2 pounds (907 g) fresh spinach
- 1½-inch piece fresh ginger, roughly chopped
- 5 garlic cloves, whole
- 2 fresh green chiles, roughly chopped
- 1 onion, roughly chopped
- 1 teaspoon salt
- ½ teaspoon turmeric
- 4 tomatoes, finely chopped
- 1 to 2 tablespoons cornstarch to thicken (if required)
- 4 tablespoons butter
- 1 teaspoon cumin seeds
- 3 garlic cloves, minced
- 1 tablespoon dried fenugreek leaves
- 2 tablespoons rapeseed oil
- 12 ounces (340 g) paneer, cut into cubes

1. Set the Ninja Foodi PossibleCooker to high and add the spinach, ginger, garlic, chiles, onion, salt, turmeric, and tomatoes. 2. Cover and let it cook on high for 3 hours, or on low for 6 hours. 3. Once cooked, use an immersion blender or food processor to purée the mixture until you achieve a smooth, glossy consistency. If it appears too watery, you can thicken it on the stove or use the Ninja Foodi PossibleCooker's boil function. Alternatively, sprinkle some cornstarch to help thicken it. 4. In a separate pan, heat butter and add cumin seeds, letting them sizzle. Then, add the minced garlic and sauté until lightly browned. Remove from heat, stir in dried fenugreek leaves, and mix this into the saag in the Ninja Foodi PossibleCooker. 5. In the same pan, fry the paneer cubes in a bit of oil until golden brown, then add them to the saag. Cover and let everything sit for an additional 10 minutes before serving.

Hearty Ninja Foodi PossibleCooker Ratatouille

Prep time: 20 minutes | Cook time: 4 to 7 hours | Serves 6

- 1 tablespoon olive oil
- 1 large onion, chopped
- 6 large garlic cloves, minced
- 1 green bell pepper, cut into strips
- 1 red bell pepper, cut into strips
- 1 medium eggplant, cubed
- 2 cups thickly sliced mushrooms
- 4 tomatoes, cubed
- 1 cup low-sodium tomato purée
- ¼ cup dry red wine or wine vinegar
- 1 tablespoon lemon juice
- 2 teaspoons dried thyme
- 1 teaspoon dried oregano
- 1 teaspoon ground cumin
- ½ to 1 teaspoon salt
- ¼ to ½ teaspoon black pepper
- 4 tablespoons minced fresh basil
- ¼ cup chopped fresh parsley

1. Turn Ninja Foodi PossibleCooker on high for 2 minutes. 2. Pour oil into Ninja Foodi PossibleCooker and add remaining ingredients except parsley and fresh basil. 3. Cover. Cook on high 2 hours, then on low 4 to 5 hours. 4. Stir in fresh basil. Sprinkle with parsley. Serve.

Cheesy Bacon Cauliflower Bake

Prep time: 10 minutes | Cook time: 1½ to 5 hours | Serves 4 to 6

- 2 (10-ounce / 283-g) packages frozen cauliflower, thawed
- Salt and pepper
- 1 (10¾-ounce / 305-g) can condensed Cheddar cheese soup
- 4 slices bacon, crisply fried and crumbled

1. Place cauliflower in Ninja Foodi PossibleCooker. Season with salt and pepper. 2. Spoon soup over top. Sprinkle with bacon. 3. Cover and cook on high 1½ hours, or on low 4 to 5 hours, or until cauliflower is tender.

Herb Tomatoes

Prep time: 5 minutes | Cook time: ¾ to 1 hour | Serves 4

- 2 tomatoes, each cut in half
- ½ tablespoon olive oil
- ½ teaspoon parsley, chopped, or ¼ teaspoon dry parsley
- flakes
- ¼ teaspoon dried oregano
- ¼ teaspoon dried basil
- Nonfat cooking spray

1. Place tomato halves in Ninja Foodi PossibleCooker sprayed with nonfat cooking spray. 2. Drizzle oil over tomatoes. Sprinkle with remaining ingredients. 3. Cover. Cook on high 45 minutes to 1 hour.

Easy Olive Bake

Prep time: 15 minutes | Cook time: 3 hours | Serves 8

- 1 cup rice, uncooked
- 2 medium onions, chopped
- ½ cup butter, melted
- 2 cups stewed tomatoes
- 2 cups water
- 1 cup black olives, quartered
- ½ to ¾ teaspoon salt
- ½ teaspoon chili powder
- 1 tablespoon Worcestershire sauce
- 1 (4-ounce / 113-g) can mushrooms with juice
- ½ cup shredded cheese

1. Rinse the rice thoroughly and drain it, then add it to the Ninja Foodi PossibleCooker. 2. Incorporate all the other ingredients, excluding the cheese, and mix until well combined. 3. Cook on high for 1 hour, then reduce the heat to low and continue cooking for an additional 2 hours, or until the rice is tender but not overly soft. 4. Stir in the cheese just before serving.

Velvety Broccoli & Cauliflower Bake

Prep time: 15 minutes | Cook time: 6 hours | Serves 6

- 1 tablespoon extra-virgin olive oil
- 1 pound (454 g) broccoli, cut into florets
- 1 pound (454 g) cauliflower, cut into florets
- ¼ cup almond flour
- 2 cups coconut milk
- ½ teaspoon ground nutmeg
- Pinch freshly ground black pepper
- 1½ cups shredded Gouda cheese, divided

1. Lightly grease the insert of the Ninja Foodi PossibleCooker with the olive oil. 2. Place the broccoli and cauliflower in the insert. 3. In a small bowl, stir together the almond flour, coconut milk, nutmeg, pepper, and 1 cup of the cheese. 4. Pour the coconut milk mixture over the vegetables and top the casserole with the remaining ½ cup of the cheese. 5. Cover and cook on low for 6 hours. 6. Serve warm.

Apple Praline Sweet Potato Gratin

Prep time: 20 minutes | Cook time: 7 hours | Serves 6 to 8

- 4 large sweet potatoes, peeled and cut into ½-inch-thick slices
- 2 large Granny Smith apples, peeled, cored, and cut into ½-inch-thick slices
- ½ cup (1 stick) unsalted butter, melted
- ½ cup firmly packed light brown sugar
- ¼ cup dark corn syrup
- ½ cup apple cider or apple juice
- 1 teaspoon ground cinnamon
- 1 cup pecans, toasted, for garnish

1. Lightly grease the insert of a 5- to 7-quart Ninja Foodi PossibleCooker with nonstick cooking spray or line it with a slow-cooker liner as directed. 2. Arrange the sweet potatoes and apples in the Ninja Foodi PossibleCooker. In a separate bowl, mix together the remaining ingredients (excluding the pecans) and pour this mixture over the layered fruits and vegetables. Cover and cook on low for 7 hours, or until the sweet potatoes are tender when tested with a paring knife. 3. Just before serving, sprinkle the pecans on top of the casserole. Keep the cooker on warm while serving.

Spinach Parmesan Strata

Prep time: 15 minutes | Cook time: 3 to 3½ hours | Serves 6 to 8

- 2 tablespoons unsalted butter
- 2 medium shallots, finely chopped
- 2 (16-ounce / 454-g) packages frozen chopped spinach, defrosted and drained
- ¼ teaspoon freshly grated nutmeg
- 6 large eggs
- 2 cups milk
- 1½ teaspoons salt
- 1 teaspoon Tabasco sauce
- 6 cups bread cubes, crusts removed (a sturdy bread like Pepperidge Farm)
- 1 cup freshly grated Parmesan cheese

1. Lightly grease the insert of a 5- to 7-quart Ninja Foodi PossibleCooker with nonstick cooking spray or use a slow-cooker liner as per the instructions. 2. In a medium skillet over medium-high heat, melt the butter. Add the shallots and sauté for about 2 minutes until softened. Then, stir in the spinach and nutmeg, cooking until the moisture has evaporated. Let this mixture cool. 3. In a large bowl, whisk together the eggs, milk, salt, and Tabasco. Layer half of the bread in the Ninja Foodi PossibleCooker, followed by half of the spinach mixture and half of the cheese. Repeat with the remaining bread, spinach, and cheese. Pour the egg mixture over the layers, pressing down gently to ensure the bread absorbs the liquid. Cover and cook on low for 3 to 3½ hours, or until the strata is fully cooked. 4. Serve directly from the Ninja Foodi PossibleCooker while keeping it warm.

Balsamic Glazed Brussels Sprouts with Pine Nuts

Prep time: 10 minutes | Cook time: 2 to 3 hours | Serves 4 to 6

- 1 cup balsamic vinegar
- ¼ cup honey
- 2 pounds (907 g) Brussels sprouts, trimmed and halved
- 2 cups vegetable stock
- 1 teaspoon sea salt
- Black pepper
- 2 tablespoons extra-virgin olive oil
- ¼ cup pine nuts, toasted
- ¼ cup grated Parmesan cheese

1. Mix the balsamic vinegar and honey in a small saucepan over medium-high heat. Stir constantly until the sugar has dissolved. Bring to a boil, reduce the heat to low, and simmer until the glaze is reduced by half, about 20 minutes. The glaze is finished when it will coat the back of a spoon. Set aside. 2. 2 Combine the Brussels sprouts, stock, and ½ teaspoon salt in the Ninja Foodi PossibleCooker. Cover and cook on high for 2 to 3 hours, or until the Brussels sprouts are tender. 3. Drain the Brussels sprouts and transfer to a serving dish. Season with salt and pepper. Drizzle with 2 tablespoons or more of the balsamic glaze and the olive oil, then sprinkle with the pine nuts and Parmesan. Serve hot.

Do-Ahead Mashed Potatoes

Prep time: 45 minutes | Cook time: 3 to 4 hours | Serves 8

- 12 medium potatoes, washed, peeled, and quartered
- 1 small or medium onion, chopped
- 4 ounces (113 g) fat-free
- cream cheese
- 1 teaspoon salt
- ¼ teaspoon black pepper
- 1 cup skim milk

1. In a saucepan, place the potatoes and onion and cover them with water. Bring to a boil, then reduce the heat and simmer for about 30 minutes until everything is tender. Drain well. 2. Use a potato masher to mash the potatoes and onion until mostly smooth. 3. In a large mixing bowl, combine the partially mashed mixture with cream cheese, salt, pepper, and milk. Whip the mixture on high speed for 3 minutes until creamy. 4. Spoon the mashed potato mixture into the Ninja Foodi PossibleCooker. 5. Set the cooker to low and let it cook for 3 to 4 hours.

Balsamic Glazed Baby Carrots

Prep time: 10 minutes | Cook time: 3 to 4 hours | Serves 6

- Cooking spray or 1 tablespoon extra-virgin olive oil
- 2 pounds (907 g) baby carrots
- 2 tablespoons butter, melted
- 3 sprigs fresh thyme
- ½ cup packed brown sugar
- ⅓ cup balsamic vinegar
- ½ teaspoon kosher salt
- ¼ teaspoon freshly ground black pepper
- ⅛ teaspoon ground cinnamon

1. Use the cooking spray or olive oil to coat the inside (bottom and sides) of the Ninja Foodi PossibleCooker. Add the carrots, butter, and thyme to the Ninja Foodi PossibleCooker. Stir to combine. Cover and cook on low for 3 to 4 hours, or until tender. Discard the thyme sprigs. 2. Meanwhile, mix together the brown sugar, vinegar, salt, pepper, and cinnamon. Add the mixture to the Ninja Foodi PossibleCooker and toss with the carrots before serving.

Uptown Scalloped Potatoes

Prep time: 15 minutes | Cook time: 6 to 7 hours | Serves 8 to 10

- 5 pounds (2.3 kg) red potatoes, peeled and sliced
- 2 cups water
- 1 teaspoon cream of tartar
- ¼ pound (113 g) bacon, cut
- in 1-inch squares, browned until crisp, and drained
- Dash of salt
- ½ pint whipping cream
- 1 pint half-and-half

1. Rinse the potatoes and toss them in a bowl with water and cream of tartar, then drain well. 2. In a large Ninja Foodi PossibleCooker, create layers of potatoes and bacon, seasoning each layer with salt. 3. In a separate bowl, combine the whipping cream and half-and-half, mixing well. 4. Pour the cream mixture over the layered ingredients in the Ninja Foodi PossibleCooker. Cover and cook on low for 6 to 7 hours, or until the potatoes are tender.

Zesty Chipotle Creamer Potatoes

Prep time: 10 minutes | Cook time: 8 hours | Serves 1 cup

- 2 pounds (907 g) creamer potatoes
- 1 onion, chopped
- 3 garlic cloves, minced
- 1 chipotle chile in adobo sauce, minced
- 2 tablespoons freshly
- squeezed lemon juice
- 2 tablespoons water
- 1 tablespoon chili powder
- ½ teaspoon ground cumin
- ½ teaspoon salt
- ⅛ teaspoon freshly ground black pepper

1. In the Ninja Foodi PossibleCooker, combine all the ingredients and stir. 2. Cover and cook on low for 7 to 8 hours, or until the potatoes are tender, and serve.

Maple Chipotle–Glazed Sweets

Prep time: 15 minutes | Cook time: 4 hours | Serves 6 to 8

- 8 medium sweet potatoes, peeled, halved lengthwise, and cut into wedges
- 2 tablespoons unsalted butter, melted
- 2 tablespoons canola oil
- 4 chipotle chiles in adobo, minced
- ¼ cup maple syrup

1. Lightly spray the inside of a 5- to 7-quart Ninja Foodi PossibleCooker with nonstick cooking spray or line it as recommended by the manufacturer. 2. Place the sweet potato wedges in the Ninja Foodi PossibleCooker. In a separate bowl, mix together the remaining ingredients, then drizzle this mixture over the potatoes, stirring to ensure they are evenly coated. 3. Cover and cook on high for 4 hours, or until the wedges are tender when tested with a knife. 4. Serve the sweet potatoes warm directly from the cooker.

Party Mashed Potatoes

Prep time: 20 minutes | Cook time: 12 to 16 hours | Serves 12

- 15 medium potatoes
- 1 cup sour cream
- 1 small onion, diced fine
- 1 teaspoon salt
- ⅛ to ¼ teaspoon pepper, according to your taste
- preference
- 1 to 2 cups buttermilk
- 1 cup fresh, chopped spinach (optional)
- 1 cup shredded Colby or Cheddar cheese (optional)

1. Peel and quarter potatoes. Place in Ninja Foodi PossibleCooker. Barely cover with water. 2. Cover. Cook on low 8 to 10 hours. Drain water. 3. Mash potatoes. Add remaining ingredients except cheese. 4. Cover. Heat on low 4 to 6 hours. 5. Sprinkle with cheese 5 minutes before serving.

Herbed Potatoes

Prep time: 10 minutes | Cook time: 2½ to 3 hours | Serves 6

- 1½ pounds (680 g) small new potatoes
- ¼ cup water
- ¼ cup butter, melted
- 3 tablespoons chopped fresh parsley
- 1 tablespoon lemon juice
- 1 tablespoon chopped fresh
- chives
- 1 tablespoon dill weed
- ¼ to ½ teaspoon salt, according to your taste preference
- ⅛ to ¼ teaspoon pepper, according to your taste preference

1. Clean the potatoes and peel a strip around the middle of each. Place them in the Ninja Foodi PossibleCooker. 2. Add water to cover the potatoes. 3. Cover and cook on high for 2½ to 3 hours. Once cooked, drain the potatoes well. 4. In a saucepan, melt butter and mix in parsley, lemon juice, chives, dill, salt, and pepper. Pour this mixture over the drained potatoes. 5. Serve warm.

Ultimate Mashed Potatoes

Prep time: 15 minutes | Cook time: 3 to 4 hours | Serves 8

- 8 large russet baking potatoes, peeled and cut into 1-inch chunks
- 4 tablespoons (½ stick) unsalted butter
- ½ cup freshly grated Parmesan cheese
- 1 (8-ounce / 227-g) package cream cheese, softened
- 1 cup sour cream
- ¼ cup finely chopped fresh chives (optional)
- Salt and freshly ground black pepper

1. Prepare the insert of a 5- to 7-quart Ninja Foodi PossibleCooker by spraying it with nonstick cooking spray or lining it as per the manufacturer's instructions. 2. Boil the potatoes in salted water until they are fork-tender. 3. Drain the potatoes well, then place them in a mixing bowl. Add 2 tablespoons of butter, ¼ cup of Parmesan cheese, cream cheese, and sour cream. Mix until the texture is light and fluffy. Fold in the chives, if desired, and season with salt and pepper to taste. 4. Spoon the potato mixture into the Ninja Foodi PossibleCooker, topping it with the remaining 2 tablespoons of butter and ¼ cup of Parmesan. Set to cook on low for 3 to 4 hours, or until the butter is melted and the potatoes are heated through. 5. Serve the warm potatoes directly from the cooker.

Herb-Stuffed Ninja Foodi PossibleCooker Artichokes

Prep time: 30 minutes | Cook time: 5 hours | Serves 6

- ½ cup extra-virgin olive oil
- 1½ cups dry white wine or vermouth
- 2 cloves garlic, peeled
- 6 black peppercorns
- Juice of 1 lemon
- 6 large globe artichokes, tough outer leaves peeled away, stems trimmed flush with the bottom
- 4 cups fresh bread crumbs
- ½ cup grated Parmesan cheese
- 1½ cups grated Romano cheese
- 4 cloves garlic, minced
- Grated zest of 1 lemon
- ¼ cup finely chopped fresh basil
- ¼ cup finely chopped fresh Italian parsley
- 1 teaspoon freshly ground black pepper

1. Combine ¼ cup of the oil, the wine, garlic, peppercorns, and lemon juice in the insert of a 5- to 7-quart Ninja Foodi PossibleCooker. Using your fingers, loosen the artichoke leaves so there are spaces for the stuffing between them. Combine the bread crumbs, cheeses, garlic, lemon zest, basil, parsley, and pepper in a small bowl. 2. Push the stuffing, using a spoon, into the spaces between the leaves; the artichokes will begin to get fatter the more stuffing you put in. Arrange the artichokes in the slow-cooker insert and drizzle with the remaining ¼ cup oil. Cover and cook on low for 5 hours, until a leaf can be easily released and the artichoke heart is tender when pierced with the tip of a sharp knife. 3. Serve the artichokes warm or at room temperature as a first course or a side dish.

Herbed Cherry Tomatoes

Prep time: 10 minutes | Cook time: 1½ to 3 hours | Serves 6

- ½ cup extra-virgin olive oil
- 6 cloves garlic, sliced
- 2 teaspoons dried tarragon
- 1 teaspoon dried chervil
- ½ teaspoon dried dill
- 6 cups varicolored cherry or pear tomatoes

1. Combine all the ingredients in the insert of a 5- to 7-quart Ninja Foodi PossibleCooker. Cover and cook on high for 1½ hours or on low for 3 hours. 2. Serve the tomatoes at room temperature.

Garlic Potatoes

Prep time: 10 minutes | Cook time: 5 to 6 hours | Serves 6

- 6 potatoes, peeled and cubed
- 6 garlic cloves, minced
- ¼ cup dried onion, or 1 medium onion, chopped
- 2 tablespoons olive oil

1. Combine all ingredients in Ninja Foodi PossibleCooker. 2. Cook on low 5 to 6 hours, or until potatoes are soft but not turning brown.

Maple-Glazed Sweet Potatoes

Prep time: 10 minutes | Cook time: 7 to 9 hours | Serves 5

- 5 medium sweet potatoes, cut in ½-inch-thick slices
- ¼ cup brown sugar, packed
- ¼ cup pure maple syrup
- ¼ cup apple cider
- 2 tablespoons butter

1. Place potatoes in Ninja Foodi PossibleCooker. 2. In a small bowl, combine brown sugar, maple syrup, and apple cider. Mix well. Pour over potatoes. Stir until all potato slices are covered. 3. Cover and cook on low 7 to 9 hours, or until potatoes are tender. 4. Stir in butter before serving.

Green Bean Casserole Supreme

Prep time: 30 minutes | Cook time: 1 to 2 hours | Serves 12 to 14

- 4 (14½-ounce / 411-g) cans green beans, drained
- 1 (10¾-ounce / 305-g) can cream of mushroom soup
- 1 (14½-ounce / 411-g) can chicken broth
- 1 cup tater tots
- 1 (3-ounce / 85-g) can French-fried onion rings

1. Put green beans in Ninja Foodi PossibleCooker. 2. In a bowl, mix soup and broth together. Spread over beans. 3. Spoon tater tots over all. Top with onion rings. 4. Cover and cook on high 1 to 2 hours, or until heated through and potatoes are cooked.

Apple-Glazed Carrots

Prep time: 10 minutes | Cook time: 2½ to 3½ hours | Serves 4

- 1 (16-ounce / 454-g) package frozen baby carrots
- ¼ cup apple cider or apple juice
- ¼ cup apple jelly
- 1½ teaspoons Dijon mustard

1. Place the carrots in the Ninja Foodi PossibleCooker and pour apple juice over them. 2. Cover and cook on high for 2 to 3 hours, or until the carrots are tender. 3. In a small bowl, mix together the apple jelly and mustard until well blended. 4. During the last 45 minutes of cooking, stir the jelly mixture into the carrots and continue cooking until everything is steaming hot.

Sweet Potato Gratin

Prep time: 15 minutes | Cook time: 4 hours | Serves 12

- 1 tablespoon butter, at room temperature
- 1 large sweet onion, such as Vidalia, thinly sliced
- 2 pounds (907 g) sweet potatoes, peeled and thinly sliced
- 1 tablespoon all-purpose flour
- 1 teaspoon chopped fresh thyme
- ½ teaspoon sea salt
- ½ teaspoon black pepper
- 2 ounces (57 g) grated fresh Parmesan cheese
- Nonstick cooking oil spray
- ½ cup vegetable stock

1. In a medium nonstick skillet, melt the butter over medium heat. Add the onion and sauté for about 5 minutes, or until lightly browned, then transfer to a large bowl. 2. In the same bowl, combine the sweet potatoes, flour, thyme, salt, pepper, and half of the grated Parmesan cheese. Toss gently to coat the sweet potato slices with the flour mixture. 3. Spray the Ninja Foodi PossibleCooker with cooking oil spray, then transfer the sweet potato mixture into it. 4. Pour the stock over the mixture and sprinkle with the remaining Parmesan. Cover and cook on low for 4 hours, or until the potatoes are tender. Serve hot.

Herb-Buttered Fingerling Potatoes

Prep time: 15 minutes | Cook time: 4 to 5 hours | Serves 6

- 2½ pounds (1.1 kg) fingerling potatoes, scrubbed and cut in half
- ½ cup (1 stick) unsalted butter, melted
- ¼ cup olive oil
- 6 fresh sage leaves, finely chopped
- 1½ teaspoons salt
- ½ teaspoon freshly ground black pepper
- ¼ cup finely chopped fresh Italian parsley, for garnish
- ¼ cup freshly grated Parmesan cheese, for garnish

1. Put the potatoes in the insert of a 5- to 7-quart Ninja Foodi PossibleCooker. Add the butter, oil, sage, salt, and pepper and stir to distribute the ingredients. Cover and cook on low for 4 to 5 hours, until the potatoes are tender. 2. Combine the parsley and cheese in a small bowl and sprinkle over the top of the potatoes. 3. Serve the potatoes immediately.

Pizza Potatoes

Prep time: 15 minutes | Cook time: 6 to 10 hours | Serves 4 to 6

- 6 medium potatoes, sliced
- 1 large onion, thinly sliced
- 2 tablespoons olive oil
- 2 cups shredded Mozzarella cheese
- 2 ounces (57 g) sliced pepperoni
- 1 teaspoon salt
- 1 (8-ounce / 227-g) can pizza sauce

1. In a skillet, sauté sliced potatoes and onions in oil until the onions become transparent. Drain well. 2. In a Ninja Foodi PossibleCooker, combine the sautéed potatoes, onions, cheese, pepperoni, and salt. 3. Pour pizza sauce over the mixture. 4. Cover and cook on low for 6 to 10 hours, or until the potatoes are tender.

Maple-Glazed Sweet Potatoes & Apples

Prep time: 15 minutes | Cook time: 6 to 8 hours | Serves 8 to 10

- 3 large sweet potatoes, peeled and cubed
- 3 large tart and firm apples, peeled and sliced
- ½ to ¾ teaspoon salt
- ⅛ to ¼ teaspoon pepper
- 1 teaspoon sage
- 1 teaspoon ground cinnamon
- 4 tablespoons (½ stick) butter, melted
- ¼ cup maple syrup
- Toasted sliced almonds or chopped pecans (optional)

1. Place half the sweet potatoes in Ninja Foodi PossibleCooker. Layer in half the apple slices. 2. Mix together seasonings. Sprinkle half over apples. 3. Mix together butter and maple syrup. Spoon half over seasonings. 4. Repeat layers. 5. Cover. Cook on low 6 to 8 hours or until potatoes are soft, stirring occasionally. 6. To add a bit of crunch, sprinkle with toasted almonds or pecans when serving. 7. Serve.

Zucchini in Sour Cream

Prep time: 10 minutes | Cook time: 1 to 1½ hours | Serves 6

- 4 cups unpeeled, sliced zucchini
- 1 cup fat-free sour cream
- ¼ cup skim milk
- 1 cup chopped onions
- 1 teaspoon salt
- 1 cup shredded low-fat sharp Cheddar cheese
- Nonfat cooking spray

1. Parboil the zucchini in the microwave for 2 to 3 minutes, then transfer to a Ninja Foodi PossibleCooker sprayed with nonfat cooking spray. 2. In a bowl, mix together the sour cream, milk, onions, and salt. Pour this mixture over the zucchini and stir gently to combine. 3. Cover the Ninja Foodi PossibleCooker and cook on low for 1 to 1½ hours. 4. About 30 minutes before serving, sprinkle cheese over the vegetables and allow to melt.

Roasted Beets with Goat Cheese and Pomegranate Dressing

Prep time: 15 minutes | Cook time: 5 hours | Serves 6 to 8

- 6 to 8 medium beets, scrubbed, stem ends trimmed
- 1 cup canola or vegetable oil
- ½ cup pomegranate juice
- ¼ cup rice vinegar
- 2 shallots, finely chopped
- 2 teaspoons sugar
- 1 teaspoon salt
- ½ teaspoon freshly ground black pepper
- ¼ cup thinly sliced fresh basil, for garnish
- 8 ounces (227 g) goat cheese, crumbled, for garnish

1. Wrap each beet in aluminum foil and place them in the insert of a 5- to 7-quart Ninja Foodi PossibleCooker. Cover and cook on high for about 5 hours, or until a knife easily pierces the thickest part of the beet. 2. Once cooked, remove the beets and let them cool. Unwrap and peel off the skins using a sharp paring knife. 3. Cut the beets into wedges and transfer them to a bowl. In a separate bowl, whisk together the oil, pomegranate juice, vinegar, shallots, sugar, salt, and pepper. Pour this dressing over the beets and toss to coat. 4. Let the beets marinate for at least 2 hours or up to 3 days in the refrigerator. 5. Before serving, drain the beets and arrange them on a platter, garnishing with fresh basil and crumbled goat cheese.

Chapter
9
Desserts

Chapter 9 Desserts

Bananas Foster Delight

Prep time: 10 minutes | Cook time: 1¼ hours | Serves 8

- Nonstick cooking oil spray
- 1 cup dark brown sugar
- ¼ cup butter
- ¼ cup dark rum
- ¼ cup banana liqueur
- ½ teaspoon ground cinnamon
- 4 ripe bananas, cut in half lengthwise, then halved crosswise
- 2 cups vanilla ice cream, for serving

1. Coat the interior of the Ninja Foodi PossibleCooker crock with nonstick cooking oil spray. 2. Combine the brown sugar, butter, rum, and banana liqueur in the Ninja Foodi PossibleCooker. 3. Cover and cook on low for 1 hour. Stir the sauce with a whisk until smooth. 4. Add the cinnamon and bananas to the sauce, and spoon the sauce over to coat. Cover and cook on low for 15 minutes. 5. Serve hot with a scoop of ice cream.

Blueberry Cornmeal Buckle

Prep time: 25 minutes | Cook time: 3½ hours | Serves 6 to 8

- Nonstick baking spray
Batter:
- 1¼ cups all-purpose flour
- ¾ cup fine yellow cornmeal
- 1½ teaspoons baking powder
- ¼ teaspoon baking soda
- 2 teaspoon coarse salt
- ½ cup (1 stick) unsalted butter, room temperature
Streusel:
- ½ cup all-purpose flour
- 3 tablespoons light brown sugar
- 1 cup granulated sugar
- 2 teaspoon vanilla extract
- 2 large eggs
- ¾ cup buttermilk, preferably full-fat
- 1 cup blueberries

- 3 tablespoons unsalted butter, room temperature
- ½ teaspoon ground cinnamon

1. Lightly coat the insert of a 4-quart Ninja Foodi PossibleCooker with baking spray. Line bottom with parchment and spray. Make the Batter: 2. Whisk together flour, cornmeal, baking powder, baking soda, and salt in a bowl. With an electric mixer on medium, beat butter, sugar, and vanilla until pale and fluffy, 3 to 5 minutes. Beat in eggs, one at a time. Add flour mixture in three batches, alternating with buttermilk; beat until combined. 3. Transfer batter to Ninja Foodi PossibleCooker; smooth top with an offset spatula. Top with blueberries. Wrap lid with a clean kitchen towel, gathering the ends at top (to absorb condensation). Cover and cook on high for 2 hours (or on low for 4 hours); cake will be undercooked. Rotate halfway through for even baking. Make the Streusel: 4. In a small bowl, combine flour, brown sugar, butter, and cinnamon. Using a fork, mix butter into flour mixture until fine crumbs form. Using your hands, squeeze together the mixture to form large clumps. 5. Scatter streusel on top of cake, concentrating mixture around edges. Cover and cook on high until a tester inserted in center comes out clean, 1 to 1½ hours longer (or on low for 2 to 3 hours). Cool in pan for 15 minutes, then invert onto a cutting board; invert again onto a wire rack to cool completely, right side up.

Perfect Crème Brûlée

Prep time: 10 minutes | Cook time: 1½ to 2 hours | Serves 6 to 8

- 8 to 10 cups boiling water
- 3½ cups heavy cream
- ⅔ cup superfine sugar
- 10 large egg yolks
- 1 tablespoon vanilla bean paste
- ¼ cup raw sugar

1. Place a rack in the bottom of a 5- to 7-quart Ninja Foodi PossibleCooker and arrange 8 (4-ounce) ramekins nearby. 2. Pour boiling water into the cooker until it reaches halfway up the sides of the ramekins when added later. Cover the cooker to keep the water hot. 3. In a large mixing bowl, whisk together the cream, superfine sugar, and egg yolks until smooth. Stir in the vanilla bean paste until well combined. Carefully pour the custard mixture into the ramekins, cover each with aluminum foil, and place them on the rack in the Ninja Foodi PossibleCooker. 4. Cover and cook on high for 1½ to 2 hours, until the custards are set (they may jiggle slightly in the center but will firm up as they cool). Remove the lid and let the custards cool slightly. Replace the foil with plastic wrap and refrigerate until chilled. 5. Just before serving, sprinkle raw sugar over each custard. Using a torch or broiler, heat the sugar until it bubbles and caramelizes. If broiling, do a few at a time for best results. 6. Allow to cool slightly before serving.

Creme Brulee

Prep time: 15 minutes | Cook time: 2½ hours | Serves 8

- Boiling water, for Ninja Foodi PossibleCooker
- 4 cups heavy cream
- ¾ cup granulated sugar
- 1 vanilla bean, split

- lengthwise and seeds scraped
- 7 large egg yolks
- ¼ teaspoon coarse salt
- ½ cup superfine sugar, for topping

1. Set a 1½-quart souffle dish into a 5- to 6-quart Ninja Foodi PossibleCooker. Pour enough boiling water into Ninja Foodi PossibleCooker to reach halfway up the sides of souffle dish. 2. Combine cream, 6 tablespoons granulated sugar, and vanilla bean and seeds into a saucepan and heat over medium just until bubbles start to form around edges, 7 to 8 minutes (do not boil). 3. Whisk yolks with remaining 6 tablespoons granulated sugar and the salt, in a large bowl. Gently whisk a small amount of cream mixture into egg mixture to combine. Add 2 more ladles of cream mixture, one at a time, whisking to combine after each. Gradually whisk in remaining cream mixture. Strain custard through a fine sieve into a large measuring cup (discard solids). Pour custard into dish. 4. Cover Ninja Foodi PossibleCooker and cook on high until custard is just set, about 2½ hours (or on low for 5 hours). Turn off Ninja Foodi PossibleCooker, remove lid, and let custard stand until water is cool enough to remove dish. Let cool completely, cover with plastic wrap, and refrigerate, at least 2 hours and up to 3 days. 5. Sprinkle superfine sugar over custard. Pass the flame of a kitchen torch in a circular motion 1 to 2 inches above custard until sugar bubbles and turns amber. Serve immediately.

Amaretto Almond Pear Crumble

Prep time: 10 minutes | Cook time: 2½ hours | Serves 8

- 1 cup firmly packed light brown sugar
- ¼ cup amaretto liqueur
- ¾ cup (1½ sticks) unsalted butter, melted
- 8 large firm pears, peeled, cored and coarsely chopped

- ½ cup granulated sugar
- ½ cup all-purpose flour
- ¾ teaspoon ground cinnamon
- ¼ teaspoon freshly grated nutmeg
- ⅔ cup sliced almonds
- Whipped cream for serving

1. Coat the insert of a 5- to 7-quart Ninja Foodi PossibleCooker with nonstick cooking spray. Add the brown sugar, amaretto, and ½ cup of the butter to the slow-cooker insert and stir until blended. Add the pears and turn the pears to coat with the syrup. 2. Stir together the granulated sugar, flour, cinnamon, nutmeg, and almonds in a small bowl. Drizzle the remaining ¼ cup butter into the flour mixture and stir with a fork until the mixture begins to form crumbs. Sprinkle over the top of the pears. Cover and cook on high for 2½ hours, until a skewer inserted into the crumble comes out clean. Uncover and allow to cool for 30 minutes. 3. Serve the crumble warm with a dollop of whipped cream.

Very Vanilla Ninja Foodi PossibleCooker Cheesecake

Prep time: 40 minutes | Cook time: 2 hours | Serves 6

- ¾ cup graham cracker crumbs
- 1 tablespoon sugar plus ⅔ cup sugar, divided
- ¼ teaspoon ground cinnamon
- 2½ tablespoons butter, melted

Topping:
- 2 ounces (57 g) semisweet chocolate, chopped

- 2 (8-ounce / 227-g) packages cream cheese, softened
- ½ cup sour cream
- 2 to 3 teaspoons vanilla extract
- 2 eggs, lightly beaten

- 1 teaspoon shortening
- Toasted sliced almonds

1. Grease a 6-inch springform pan and place it on a double layer of heavy-duty foil (about 12 inches square), wrapping the foil securely around the pan. 2. Pour 1 inch of water into a 6-quart Ninja Foodi PossibleCooker. Create a rack by layering two 24-inch pieces of aluminum foil, rolling them into a 1-inch-wide strip, and shaping it into a circle to place at the bottom of the Ninja Foodi PossibleCooker. 3. In a small bowl, mix together cracker crumbs, 1 tablespoon of sugar, and cinnamon. Stir in melted butter and press the mixture into the bottom and about 1 inch up the sides of the prepared pan. 4. In a large bowl, beat the cream cheese and remaining sugar until smooth. Add sour cream and vanilla, then beat in the eggs on low speed just until combined. Pour the filling into the crust. 5. Set the springform pan on the foil circle in the Ninja Foodi PossibleCooker, ensuring it doesn't touch the sides. Cover the Ninja Foodi PossibleCooker with a double layer of paper towels, then secure the lid over the towels. Cook on high for 2 hours. 6. Do not remove the lid; turn off the Ninja Foodi PossibleCooker and let the cheesecake sit, covered, for 1 hour. 7. Carefully remove the springform pan from the cooker and take off the foil. Allow the cheesecake to cool on a wire rack for 1 additional hour. Loosen the sides with a knife and refrigerate overnight, covering once completely cooled. 8. For the topping, melt chocolate and shortening in the microwave, stirring until smooth. Let cool slightly, then pour over the cheesecake and sprinkle with almonds before serving.

"Baked" Stuffed Apples

Prep time: 15 minutes | Cook time: 2½ to 5 hours | Serves 6 to 8

- 2 tablespoons raisins
- ¼ cup sugar
- 6 to 8 medium baking apples, cored but left whole
- and unpeeled
- 1 teaspoon ground cinnamon
- 2 tablespoons butter
- ½ cup water

1. In a small bowl, combine raisins and sugar. 2. Place the apples upright at the bottom of the Ninja Foodi PossibleCooker and fill each apple's center with the raisin-sugar mixture, dividing it evenly. 3. Sprinkle cinnamon over the stuffed apples and add small pieces of butter on top. 4. Pour ½ cup of water around the edges of the Ninja Foodi PossibleCooker. 5. Cover and cook on low for 3 to 5 hours or on high for 2½ to 3½ hours, until the apples are tender but not collapsing. 6. Serve warm.

Slow-Stewed Dried Fruit Medley

Prep time: 5 minutes | Cook time: 4 to 8 hours | Serves 3 to 4

- 2 cups mixed dried fruit
- ¼ cup water

1. Place dried fruit in Ninja Foodi PossibleCooker. Add water. 2. Cover. Cook on low 4 to 8 hours. 3. Serve warm.

Maple Creme Brulee

Prep time: 20 minutes | Cook time: 2 hours | Serves 3

- 1⅓ cups heavy whipping cream
- 3 egg yolks

Topping:

- 1½ teaspoons sugar
- ½ cup packed brown sugar
- ¼ teaspoon ground cinnamon
- ½ teaspoon maple flavoring
- 1½ teaspoons brown sugar

1. In a small saucepan, gently heat the cream until it starts to bubble around the edges. In a separate bowl, whisk together the egg yolks, brown sugar, and cinnamon. Gradually add a small amount of the hot cream to the egg mixture to temper it, then return the mixture to the saucepan, stirring constantly. Stir in the maple flavoring. 2. Pour the mixture into three 6-ounce ramekins. Place the ramekins in a 6-quart Ninja Foodi PossibleCooker and add enough boiling water to reach about 1 inch up the sides of the ramekins. Cover and cook on high for 2 to 2½ hours, or until the centers are just set and jiggle slightly. Carefully remove the ramekins and let them cool for 10 minutes, then cover and refrigerate for at least 4 hours. 3. For the topping, mix together granulated sugar and brown sugar. If using a kitchen torch, sprinkle the sugar mixture over the chilled custards and caramelize with the torch until bubbly and golden. Serve immediately. 4. If you prefer to broil the custards, place the ramekins on a baking sheet and let them sit at room temperature for 15 minutes. Sprinkle with the sugar mixture and broil 8 inches from the heat for 3 to 5 minutes, until the sugar caramelizes. Allow to cool in the refrigerator for 1 to 2 hours until firm before serving.

Five-Spice Poached Asian Pears

Prep time: 10 minutes | Cook time: 2½ hours | Serves 8

- ½ cup (1 stick) unsalted butter, melted
- 1½ cups firmly packed light brown sugar
- ½ cup dry sherry
- 1 teaspoon five-spice powder
- 1 cup pear nectar
- 8 firm pears, peeled, halved, and cored

1. Mix together the butter, sugar, sherry, five-spice powder, and pear nectar in the insert of a 5- to 7-quart Ninja Foodi PossibleCooker. Add the pears to the slow-cooker insert and turn to coat them with the liquid. Cover and cook on high for 2½ hours until tender. 2. Remove the pears with a slotted spoon to a serving bowl and spoon the liquid from the Ninja Foodi PossibleCooker over the pears. Serve warm or chilled.

Apple-Pear Sauce

Prep time: 20 minutes | Cook time: 8 hours | Makes 8 cups

- Nonstick cooking spray
- 4 apples, peeled and sliced
- 3 firm pears, peeled and sliced
- ¼ cup apple cider
- ½ cup granulated sugar
- 2 tablespoons freshly squeezed lemon juice
- 1 teaspoon ground cinnamon
- 1 teaspoon ground nutmeg
- ⅛ teaspoon salt
- 1 teaspoon vanilla

1. Lightly spray the Ninja Foodi PossibleCooker with nonstick cooking spray. 2. Add the chopped apples and pears to the cooker, stirring to combine. 3. Pour in the apple cider, sugar, lemon juice, cinnamon, nutmeg, and salt, mixing well. 4. Cover and cook on low for 7 to 8 hours, or until the fruit is very soft. 5. Once cooked, mash the mixture to your desired consistency using a fork or potato masher. Stir in the vanilla extract and transfer to a serving dish. 6. Serve warm or let cool before refrigerating for up to 4 days or freezing for later use.

Classic Tapioca Pudding Delight

Prep time: 10 minutes | Cook time: 2½ hours | Serves 6 to 8

- 3 cups whole milk
- 1 cup heavy cream
- 1¼ cups sugar
- ½ cup pearl tapioca (not instant)
- Grated zest of 1 orange
- 2 large eggs, beaten
- 1 teaspoon vanilla paste or vanilla extract

1. Coat the insert of a 5- to 7-quart Ninja Foodi PossibleCooker with nonstick cooking spray. Whisk together the milk, cream, and sugar in a bowl. Pour into the slow-cooker insert, then sprinkle the tapioca evenly over the top. 2. Cover and cook on low for 2 hours; the tapioca should be transparent. Stir the orange zest into the beaten eggs in a small bowl. 3. Remove the cover from the Ninja Foodi PossibleCooker and stir the eggs and vanilla paste into the tapioca. 4. Cover and cook for an additional 30 minutes, until the milk is absorbed. Remove the cover and let the pudding cool for 30 to 0 minutes. 5. Serve warm or chilled.

Cherries Jubilee Chocolate Lava Cake

Prep time: 20 minutes | Cook time: 2 hours | Serves 4 to 6

Cherries:

- 2 (16-ounce / 454-g) bags frozen unsweetened pitted sweet cherries, defrosted and drained

Chocolate Cake:

- ½ cup milk
- 3 tablespoons unsalted butter, melted
- 1 teaspoon vanilla bean paste
- 1 cup granulated sugar
- 1 cup all-purpose flour
- ¼ cup sugar
- 2 tablespoons cornstarch
- 2 tablespoons brandy or Grand Marnier
- ½ cup cocoa powder (make sure to use natural cocoa powder, not Dutch process)
- 2 teaspoons baking powder
- ¾ cup firmly packed light brown sugar
- 1¼ cups boiling water

1. Coat the insert for a 3½- to 4-quart Ninja Foodi PossibleCooker with nonstick cooking spray. Add all the cherries, sugar, cornstarch, and brandy to the slow-cooker insert and stir to combine. 2. Stir together the milk, butter, and vanilla bean paste in a mixing bowl. Gradually stir in the granulated sugar, flour, ¼ cup of the cocoa powder, and the baking powder. 3. Spread the batter evenly over the cherries in the slow-cooker insert. Mix together the brown sugar and remaining ¼ cup cocoa powder in a small bowl and sprinkle evenly over the batter. Pour in the boiling water (do not stir). 4. Cover and cook on high for 2 hours, until a skewer inserted into the center comes out clean. Uncover and allow to cool for about 20 minutes. 5. Serve spooned from the Ninja Foodi PossibleCooker, so the cherries are a surprise resting on top of the cake.

Low-Fat Apple Cake

Prep time: 15 minutes | Cook time: 2½ to 3 hours | Serves 8

- 1 cup flour
- ¾ cup sugar
- 2 teaspoons baking powder
- 1 teaspoon ground cinnamon
- ¼ teaspoon salt
- 4 medium cooking apples, chopped
- ⅓ cup eggbeaters
- 2 teaspoons vanilla

1. In a bowl, mix flour, sugar, baking powder, cinnamon, and salt. 2. Gently fold in the apples until coated. 3. In a separate bowl, whisk together eggbeaters and vanilla, then add to the apple mixture, stirring until just combined. Spoon the mixture into a lightly greased Ninja Foodi PossibleCooker. 4. Cover and cook on high for 2½ to 3 hours. 5. Serve warm.

Warm Lemon Blueberry Pudding Cake

Prep time: 20 minutes | Cook time: 2 to 2½ hours | Serves 6

- 1 cup fresh blueberries
- 4 large eggs, separated
- Grated zest of 1 lemon
- ⅓ cup fresh lemon juice
- 4 tablespoons (½ stick)
- butter, at room temperature
- 1⅔ cups milk
- 1 cup sugar
- ⅓ cup all-purpose flour
- ⅛ teaspoon salt

1. Coat the insert of a 5- to 7-quart Ninja Foodi PossibleCooker with nonstick cooking spray. Spread the blueberries over the bottom of the slow-cooker insert. Beat the egg whites in a large mixing bowl until soft peaks form, and set aside. 2. Whisk the egg yolks in another mixing bowl. Add the zest and juice, butter, and milk and whisk until blended. Stir together the sugar, flour, and salt in another bowl and add to the egg yolk mixture. Beat until smooth, then fold into the reserved egg whites. 3. Transfer the batter to the Ninja Foodi PossibleCooker. Cover and cook on high for 2½ hours. 4. Allow the cake to cool slightly before serving.

Creamy Rice Pudding

Prep time: 10 minutes | Cook time: 3 hours | Serves 6 to 8

- 1 teaspoon butter or ghee
- ½ cup basmati rice, washed and drained
- 2 tablespoons sugar
- ½ teaspoon green cardamom seeds, lightly crushed
- 2 green cardamom pods
- 2 tablespoons golden raisins (optional)
- 5 cups whole milk
- 2 tablespoons crushed unsalted pistachios

1. Grease the bottom and sides of your Ninja Foodi PossibleCooker with butter or ghee. 2. Add rice, sugar, cardamom seeds, cardamom pods, raisins, and milk to the Ninja Foodi PossibleCooker. 3. Cover and cook on high for 3 hours, stirring occasionally. 4. Serve hot or cold; it will thicken as it cools. Just before serving, sprinkle with chopped nuts.

Chocolate Peanut Butter Cake

Prep time: 10 minutes | Cook time: 2 to 2½ hours | Serves 8 to 10

- 2 cups dry milk chocolate cake mix
- ½ cup water
- 6 tablespoons peanut butter
- 2 eggs
- ½ cup chopped nuts

1. In a mixing bowl, combine all ingredients and beat with an electric mixer for 2 minutes until well blended. 2. Prepare a baking insert that fits inside your Ninja Foodi PossibleCooker by spraying it with nonstick cooking spray and lightly dusting it with flour. Pour the batter into the prepared insert. 3. Cover the insert with 8 paper towels to absorb moisture during cooking. 4. Place the insert into the Ninja Foodi PossibleCooker and secure the lid. Cook on high for 2 to 2½ hours, checking for doneness by inserting a toothpick into the center; it should come out clean. 5. Once baked, allow the cake to cool in the insert for a few minutes before inverting it onto a serving plate. Slice and serve as desired.

Honey-Glazed Cherry-Stuffed Apples

Prep time: 15 minutes | Cook time: 4 hours | Serves 2

- 3 apples
- 1 tablespoon freshly squeezed lemon juice
- ⅓ cup dried cherries
- 2 tablespoons apple cider
- 2 tablespoons honey
- ¼ cup water

1. Cut about half an inch off the top of each of the apples, and peel a small strip of the skin away around the top. 2. Using a small serrated spoon or melon baller, core the apples, making sure not to go through the bottom. Drizzle with the lemon juice. 3. Fill the apples with the dried cherries. Carefully spoon the cider and honey into the apples. 4. Place the apples in the Ninja Foodi PossibleCooker. Pour the water around the apples. 5. Cover and cook on low for 4 hours, or until the apples are soft, and serve.

Cranberry Pudding

Prep time: 20 minutes | Cook time: 3 to 4 hours | Serves 8 to 10

Pudding:

- 1⅓ cups flour
- ½ teaspoon salt
- 2 teaspoons baking soda
- ⅓ cup boiling water

Butter Sauce:

- 1 cup confectioners sugar
- ½ cup heavy cream or evaporated milk

- ½ cup dark molasses
- 2 cups whole cranberries
- ½ cup chopped nuts
- ½ cup water

- ½ cup butter
- 1 teaspoon vanilla

1. In a mixing bowl, combine the flour and salt thoroughly. 2. In a separate bowl, dissolve the baking soda in boiling water, then pour this mixture into the flour and salt mixture. 3. Stir in the molasses until well blended. 4. Gently fold in the cranberries and nuts until evenly distributed. 5. Grease and flour a bread or cake pan that fits inside your Ninja Foodi PossibleCooker, then pour the batter into the pan. Cover the top with greased aluminum foil. 6. Add ½ cup of water to the Ninja Foodi PossibleCooker, place the foil-covered pan inside, and cover the cooker with its lid. Steam on high for 3 to 4 hours, or until a wooden pick inserted into the center comes out clean. 7. Carefully remove the pan from the cooker and uncover it. Allow the pudding to sit for 5 minutes before unmolding. 8. For the butter sauce, combine all ingredients in a saucepan and cook over medium heat, stirring until the sugar has completely dissolved.

Brownies with Nuts

Prep time: 15 minutes | Cook time: 3 hours | Makes 24 brownies

- Half a stick butter, melted
- 1 cup chopped nuts, divided

- 1 (23-ounce / 652-g) package brownie mix

1. Start by greasing a baking insert that fits inside your Ninja Foodi PossibleCooker with melted butter, ensuring the sides are well-coated. 2. Evenly distribute half of the chopped nuts across the bottom of the insert. 3. In a mixing bowl, prepare the brownie batter as directed on the package. Pour half of this mixture over the nuts, making sure to cover them completely. 4. Sprinkle the remaining nuts on top, then add the rest of the brownie batter. 5. Place the baking insert into the Ninja Foodi PossibleCooker, covering it with a layer of 8 paper towels to absorb moisture. 6. Secure the lid on the Ninja Foodi PossibleCooker and set it to cook on high for 3 hours without checking until the last hour. After 2 hours, start testing for doneness by inserting a toothpick into the center; if it comes out clean, the brownies are ready. If not, continue cooking in 15-minute increments until done. 7. Once cooked, remove the lid and let the brownies cool in the insert for 5 minutes. 8. Carefully invert the insert onto a serving plate, then slice the brownies with a plastic knife to minimize crumbling. Serve them warm for the best texture.

Appendix 1: Measurement Conversion Chart

VOLUME EQUIVALENTS(DRY)

US STANDARD	METRIC (APPROXIMATE)
1/8 teaspoon	0.5 mL
1/4 teaspoon	1 mL
1/2 teaspoon	2 mL
3/4 teaspoon	4 mL
1 teaspoon	5 mL
1 tablespoon	15 mL
1/4 cup	59 mL
1/2 cup	118 mL
3/4 cup	177 mL
1 cup	235 mL
2 cups	475 mL
3 cups	700 mL
4 cups	1 L

WEIGHT EQUIVALENTS

US STANDARD	METRIC (APPROXIMATE)
1 ounce	28 g
2 ounces	57 g
5 ounces	142 g
10 ounces	284 g
15 ounces	425 g
16 ounces (1 pound)	455 g
1.5 pounds	680 g
2 pounds	907 g

VOLUME EQUIVALENTS(LIQUID)

US STANDARD	US STANDARD (OUNCES)	METRIC (APPROXIMATE)
2 tablespoons	1 fl.oz.	30 mL
1/4 cup	2 fl.oz.	60 mL
1/2 cup	4 fl.oz.	120 mL
1 cup	8 fl.oz.	240 mL
1 1/2 cup	12 fl.oz.	355 mL
2 cups or 1 pint	16 fl.oz.	475 mL
4 cups or 1 quart	32 fl.oz.	1 L
1 gallon	128 fl.oz.	4 L

TEMPERATURES EQUIVALENTS

FAHRENHEIT(F)	CELSIUS(C) (APPROXIMATE)
225 °F	107 °C
250 °F	120 °C
275 °F	135 °C
300 °F	150 °C
325 °F	160 °C
350 °F	180 °C
375 °F	190 °C
400 °F	205 °C
425 °F	220 °C
450 °F	235 °C
475 °F	245 °C
500 °F	260 °C

Appendix 2: Recipes Index

A

Acadiana BBQ Shrimp	34
Amaretto Almond Pear Crumble	79
Another Chicken in a Pot	45
Apple Bean Bake	18
Apple Kielbasa	66
Apple Praline Sweet Potato Gratin	71
Apple-Glazed Carrots	75
Apple-Pear Sauce	80
Apple-Raisin Ham	28
Applesauce-Glazed Meatballs	22
Aunt Thelma's Homemade Soup	53
Auntie Ginny's Baked Beans	16

B

Bacon-Beef Calico Bean Bake	16
Bacon-Infused Refried Beans	17
Baked Oatmeal	11
Balsamic Glazed Baby Carrots	72
"Baked" Stuffed Apples	80
Balsamic Glazed Brussels Sprouts with Pine Nuts	72
Banana Bread Breakfast Bake	12
Bananas Foster Delight	78
Barbecued Baked Beans	19
Barbecued Spoonburgers	24
Barbecued Turkey	45
Basic Strata	6
Bayou Gulf Shrimp Gumbo	34
BBQ Burgers	21
BBQ Sweet Potato Black Bean Bowl	18
Beantown Buttered Scallops	36
Beef Enchiladas	23
Beef Ribs	22
Blueberry Apple Waffle Topping	8
Blueberry Cornmeal Buckle	78
Bouillabaisse	31
Bratwurst Stew	56
Breakfast Oatmeal	11
Breakfast Prunes	9

Brownies with Nuts	83
Bulgur and Shiitake Mushroom Pilaf	15

C

Cajun Shrimp & Sausage	31
Cape Breton Chicken	47
Catalan-Style Seafood Stew	32
Cheesy Bacon Cauliflower Bake	71
Cheesy Beef and Biscuit Bake	28
Cheesy Beef Macaroni	23
Cheesy Green Chili Casserole	67
Cheesy Grits Bake	15
Cheesy Loaded Vegetable Delight	63
Cherries Jubilee Chocolate Lava Cake	81
Chet's Hearty Trucker Stew	52
Chicken and Bean Torta	46
Chicken and Shrimp Jambalaya	44
Chicken Breasts with Cornbread Stuffing	50
Chicken Cacciatore with Porcini and Cremini Mushrooms	48
Chicken Dijonaise	43
Chicken Mole	45
Chicken Stew with Gnocchi	56
Chicken Tortilla Casserole	48
Chicken with Mango Chutney	46
Chicken with Tropical Barbecue Sauce	44
Chicken-Vegetable Dish	41
Chili Nuts	68
Chili, Chicken, Corn Chowder	52
Chili-Taco Stew	55
Chinese Hamburger	23
Chinese Pot Roast	29
Chocolate Peanut Butter Cake	82
Chocolate Peanut Cluster Treats	64
Chocolate-Cherry–Stuffed French Toast	13
Cinnamon Streusel Slow-Cooker Cake	10
Citrus Swordfish	34
Classic Chicken and Homemade Dumplings	58
Classic Corned Beef and Vegetables	24
Classic Tapioca Pudding Delight	81
Classic Welsh Rarebit Dip	10

Cola-Infused Beef Roast 21

Come-Back-for-More Barbecued Chicken 46

Crab and Vegetable Soup 52

Cranberry Pudding 83

Creamy Italian Chicken 45

Creamy Rice Pudding 82

Creamy Slow-Cooked Pork Chops 23

Creamy Warm Clam Dip 66

Creme Brulee 79

Crispy Cereal-Coated Chicken 43

Crispy Snack Mix 67

Croque Monsieur Strata 6

Crunchy Keto Nut Granola 6

Curried Chicken Divan Bake 47

Curried Meatballs 26

D

Dilled Pot Roast with Creamy Sauce 25

Do-Ahead Mashed Potatoes 72

Dulce Leche 11

E

Easy Meatballs for a Group 24

Easy Olive Bake 71

F

Fajita Stew 54

Five-Spice Poached Asian Pears 80

Frittata Provencal 12

Fruited Barbecue Chicken 43

Fruity Steel-Cut Oatmeal 7

Full Meal Deal Beans 19

G

Garden Veggie Egg Hash 8

Garlic Potatoes 74

Garlic Tilapia 31

Golden Granola 7

Golden Peach Pork Chops 27

Green Bean and Ham Soup 61

Green Bean Casserole Supreme 75

Guinness-Braised Corned Beef 26

H

Halibut with Eggplant and Ginger Relish 36

Ham and Potato Chowder 60

Ham-Broccoli Casserole 28

Hamburger Vegetable Stew 59

Hearty Baked Bean Casserole 18

Hearty Beef and Veggie Casserole 24

Hearty Breakfast Risotto 10

Hearty Mixed Bean Medley 18

Hearty Mixed Bean Soup 54

Hearty Ninja Foodi PossibleCooker Ratatouille 70

Hearty Sausage and Vegetable Medley 60

Hearty Shiitake Beef Stew 28

Hearty Vegetable Soup 53

Hearty Vegetarian Chili Soup 56

Herb Tomatoes 71

Herb Turkey Breast 44

Herb-Buttered Fingerling Potatoes 75

Herbed Cherry Tomatoes 74

Herbed Potatoes 73

Herb-Infused BBQ Chicken 46

Herb-Stuffed Ninja Foodi PossibleCooker Artichokes 74

Honey Teriyaki Pork Roast 22

Honey-Glazed Cherry-Stuffed Apples 82

Honey-Lime Glazed Salmon 32

Hot Dill and Swiss Dip 68

Hot Italian Short Ribs 27

Huevos Rancheros 9

Hungarian Barley Stew 61

Hungarian Chicken 42

I

Italian Spaghetti Sauce 27

K

Karen's Hearty Split Pea Soup 57

Kidney Beans 15

L

Lamb Stew 59

Lemon Garlic Chicken and Kale Soup 59

Lemon, Garlic, and Butter Halibut 36

Loretta's Hot Chicken 46

Low Country Slow-Cooker Seafood Boil 38

Low-Fat Apple Cake 81

Low-Fat Chicken Cacciatore 49

M

Mahi-Mahi with Tropical Salsa & Lentils 33

Mango and Coconut Chicken Soup 54

Maple Chipotle–Glazed Sweets 73

Maple-Glazed Sweet Potatoes 74

Maple-Glazed Sweet Potatoes & Apples 76

Maple-Glazed Turkey Breast with Rice 49

Meatball-Barley Casserole 27

Meaty Buffet Favorites 68

Meaty Slow-Cooked Jambalaya 16

Mediterranean Beef Stew with Rosemary and Balsamic Vinegar 53

Mexican Casserole 26

Minestrone Soup 55

Mini Hot Dogs 66

Miso-Glazed Cod 39

Miso-Poached Salmon 37

Moroccan Chicken with Apricots, Almonds, and Olives 47

Moroccan Fruited Chicken Tagine 41

Moroccan-Spiced Sea Bass 35

Mushroom-Beef Stew 52

O

Oatmeal 9

Olive Oil Poached Tuna 37

One-Pot Herb Chicken Dinner 44

Osso Bucco-Style Pork Tenderloin 25

Overnight Comfort Oats 8

Overnight Oatmeal 9

P

Pacifica Sweet-Hot Salmon 32

Party Mashed Potatoes 73

Peach French Toast Bake 13

Pecos River Red-Frito Pie 23

Perfect Crème Brûlée 78

Pigs in Blankets 24

Pizza Potatoes 75

Poached Salmon Cakes in White Wine Butter Sauce 33

Poached Salmon Provenc 36

Polenta 7

Polish Sausage and Sauerkraut Stew 53

Pork and Vegetable Stew 54

Pork Chops and Stuffing with Curry 29

Potato Soup with Possibilities 55

Potato-Crusted Sea Bass Delight 34

Pumpkin Spice Breakfast Bars 12

Punjabi Chicken Curry 47

Q

Quinoa Chicken Chili 19

R

Red Wine–Marinated Sirloin 25

Refried Bean Dip 63

Reuben Spread 67

Reuben-Style Chicken Casserole 48

Rich and Creamy Potato Corn Chowder 59

Rich Cranberry-Glazed Meatballs 68

Roasted Beets with Goat Cheese and Pomegranate Dressing 76

Roasted Red Pepper and Mozzarella Stuffed Chicken Breasts 42

S

Sausage and Apples 28

Sausage Quiche 8

Savory Chex Snack Mix 66

Savory Chicken 48

Savory Curried Almonds 68

Savory Sausage Egg Bake 9

Savory Shrimp and Corn Delight 57

Savory Turkey-Style Casserole 29

Savory Wild Rice Medley 19

Savory Wild Rice Pilaf 15

Scallop & Crab Cioppino 37

Seafood Laksa 35

Shredded Chicken Chili Tacos 49

Shrimp & Artichoke Barley Risotto 32

Shrimp Marinara 38

Simple Poached Turbot 35

Slim Dunk 64

Slow-Stewed Dried Fruit Medley 80

Smoked Salmon and Potato Casserole 38

Smokies 65

Smoky BBQ Bean Bake 18

Smoky Chipotle Pulled Pork 29

South Indian Tomato and Pepper Soup 58

South-of-the-Border Halibut 39

Southwestern Chili con Queso 66

Spiced Pumpkin Pudding 10

Spiced-Pumpkin Chicken Soup 57

Spicy BBQ Scallops & Shrimp 33

Spicy Buffalo Chicken Dip 64

Spicy Crocked Nuts 65

Spicy Lamb and Herb Soup 58

Spicy Orange Chipotle Chicken Wings 67

Spicy Tomato Basil Mussels 37

Spinach and Paneer Cheese 70

Spinach Parmesan Strata 72

Split Chickpeas with Turnips 17

Stuffed Bell Peppers 21

Stuffed Peppers with Beans 70

Sunday Chicken and Dumpling Stew 56

Sunrise Fruit Compote 11

Sweet and Smoky BBQ Bites 65

Sweet and Spicy Peanuts 65

Sweet and Spicy Smoked Sausage Bites 65

Sweet Marmalade Chicken 41

Sweet Potato Chicken Shepherd's Pie 42

Sweet Potato Gratin 75

T

Taco Chicken Soup 55

Tandoori-Style Chicken 43

Tangy Barbecue Meatball Bites 63

Tangy Beef Ribs and Sauerkraut 26

Tangy Grape Jelly Meatball Bites 64

Tangy Pickled Whiting Fillets 67

Tender Turkey Breast 41

The Best Artichoke Spinach Dip on the Planet 64

Three-Bean Burrito Bake 21

Three-Cheese Vegetable Strata 11

Tiajuana Tacos 22

Tortilla Soup 60

Toscano Soup 60

Turkey with Mushroom Sauce 44

U

Ultimate All-American Snack Mix 68

Ultimate Mashed Potatoes 74

Uptown Scalloped Potatoes 73

V

Vegetable Salmon Chowder 58

Veggie Cassoulet 17

Veggie Omelet 7

Velvety Broccoli & Cauliflower Bake 71

Very Vanilla Ninja Foodi PossibleCooker Cheesecake 79

W

Warm Crab Dip 65

Warm Lemon Blueberry Pudding Cake 81

Z

Zesty Chipotle Creamer Potatoes 73

Zesty Lemon Herb Chicken 42

Zesty Mexican Rice and Bean Soup 55

Zesty Taco Pasta Soup 61

Zesty Vegetarian Chili 16

Zucchini in Sour Cream 76

42628116R00052